On
Government

SIR JOHN FORTESCUE

On Government

Edited by Simona Draghici PhD

Copyright © 1997 by PLUTARCH PRESS

Published by PLUTARCH PRESS, P.O. Box 39012
Washington, D.C. 20016-9012

ALL RIGHTS RESERVED

For information, address the publisher:
PLUTARCH PRESS, P.O. Box 39012
Washington, D.C. 20016-9012

Library of Congress Cataloging-in-Publication Data:

Fortescue, John, Sir, 1394?-1476?
    (Difference between an absolute and a limited
        monarchy)
    On Government / Sir John Fortescue; edited
        by Simona Draghici.
        p.   cm.
Originally published under the title: On the
    Monarchy of England.
    Includes bibliographical references and index.
    ISBN 0-943045-08-8 (pbk.: alk. paper)
    1. Political science--Early Works to 1800. 2.
        Monarchy--Great Brtain. 3. Great--Britain--
        Constitutional law. I. Draghici, Simona,
        1937-   . II. Title.
JC121.F73   1997
321'.6--dc21   97-8434
                                                   CIP

Manufactured in the United States of America.
Book design and cover by JAY.

TABLE OF CONTENTS

PREFACE

This edition of Sir John Fortescue's political treatise has been prepared with the student of the social sciences in mind, and particularly with the one interested in the theory, and the practice, of the modern state. As such,it is not meant to replace the 1885 edition of Charles Plummer, originally published by Clarendon Press of Oxford, and now available in a reprint from Hyperion Press of Westport, Connecticut.

Plummer approached Fortescue's text as an archivist might have done, anxious to extract from it any historiographical information it would yield. Said differently, he treated it more or less as a chronicle, adding copious notes of minutiae, especially with regard to administrative history, in order to fill the gaps which he had found unbearable,and also to correct Fortescue's alleged factual errors.

The present edition, however, is not intended to assess Fortescue's writing for its documentary accuracy, but rather to uncover the opinions of a high dignitary and practical politician about authority, force and power, social order and general well-being.

To this end, the language of the text has been modernized, given the fact that the awkward style of the surviving MSS and the printed editions has discouraged all but the historians of Lancastrian England to give it a closer look.Likewise, the Latin words, phrases and quotations scattered all over it have been translated into English. The changes are acknowledged in the notes at the back of the book.

The texts on which the present edition is based are two, both printed in the latter half of the last century: one is that included by Lord Clermont in his collection of his ancestor's works, privately printed in London in 1869, and further referred to

as "Works". The other is Plummer's, mentioned above.
Both reflect extensive collations with the earliest
available MSS, though none in Fortescue's own hand.
There are no meaningful differences between the two
printed texts, though textual ommissions and addi-
tions between them are signalled in the notes,
as well as some of the variant readings. In the process, the general title too has been changed,and the
subtitle, added by Fortescue's descendants, has been
discarded as anomalous. No sacrilege has thus been
committed, given the fact that the earliest extant
MS (Laud 593) bears no general title whatsoever, and
that the subsequent title by which Fortescue's
treatise was known, namely "Monarchia", had in all
probability been coined by John Stow, the sixteenth
century chronicler and antiquarian.
Two appendices, in modernized English, have been
added to the text proper. Appendix I was first published by Plummer in his 1885 edition of Fortescue's
treatise. It is a memorandum from which the larger
work might have evolved. Its importance lies in the
opportunity it offers to trace Fortescue's train of
thought particularly in the case of a monarch of
questionable abilities. Appendix II represents chap-
ters 24 and 25 of Book I from Fortescue's earlier
treatise, DE NATURA LEGIS NATURE (On the Nature of
the Law of Nature). They have been taken from Lord
Clermont's edition of Fortescue's writings, in the
English translation by Clermont's brother, Lord
Carlingford. The Appendix II defines and at the same
time justifies the temporary and reversible suspen-
sion of the principles of government in force,in the
conditions of a state of emergency. Thus more light
is cast upon his notion of authority,as well as upon
Fortescue's pragmatic frame of mind in matters of
practical politics. So much for the limited monarchy
his thinking has been associated with.
A select bibliography has been added which lists
texts consulted while preparing this edition. Non-

specialists might find it of some use in their attempts to grasp an age as intricate and as unstable as ours.

The idea of redressing Sir John Fortescue's reputation as a "politique" came to me while preparing a lecture on Henry VIII as a statesman, on the occasion of his 500th anniversary. A car accident delayed the completion of the project much longer than I could reckon. Here it is, finally, though short of some of my original intentions.Nonetheless, improvements can only be brought to things that exist, after all. For help throughout, I owe gratitude to the concerned and tireless staff of the Adams and the Jefferson reading-rooms of the Library of Congress and its shelf-service, headed by Bruce Martin. Finally, this edition is dedicated to the memory of two people who had provided the stimulus and the conditions to a degree, J.L. and J.F..

Washington DC   S.D.
Sept. 1991 - Nov. 1996

John Fortescue was born most likely in Devon, in the last quarter of the 14th century. He was the second son of Sir John Fortescue of Winstone, in South Devon. Father and son belonged to the new gentry.The former came to it by his prowess in war: he had been fighting at Agincourt as one of Henry V's men. The son arrived through his successful service in the most sought-after profession of the times, law. It led him to a knighthood of his own. At one time, the father was appointed military governor of the Fortress of Meaux in Brie, France, as one of the king's officers. The son, on the other hand, was eventually appointed to the highest position a common lawyer could have aspired to, at least theoretically, namely that of chief justice of the King's Bench. That happened in January 1442. He came to fill the office left vacant by the death of Sir John Hody who had held it for less than two years' time. The fact that the younger Fortescue had served only one year as king's sergeant before his 1442 appointment gives one reason to think that it was no routine promotion and relatedly, that his professional ability was only one of the criteria for his selection as chief justice of the King's Bench. The others are likely to elude the keenest researcher. It was only afterwards, as holder of that high office, though soon enough, that Fortescue was knighted. Nevertheless, one should not be left with the impression that he leaped into the limelight out of utter obscurity. Not only had he been a respected prop of of the inns of court,but also had held public office before. Thus, for instance, he had been elected to the lower house of parliament eight times before 1437, and been a justice of peace thirty-five times in seventeen counties. Almost two decades after his appointment as chief justice, in the aftermath of the lost battle of Towton, in March 1461, he hastily decided to follow the Lancastrian royal house in its procession northwards and into eventual exile abroad, firstly in Scotland, and then in France. Fortescue had been a declared enemy of Richard Duke of York, father of the future Edward IV, and it is probable that fear of Yorkist revenge weighed more than any loyalty to Henry VI, in his decision to abandon family and personal property in a hurry, without adequate provisions for those left behind. A letter of introduction to the Court of France, issued to him while he was in Scotland, describes him as chancellor of the Lancastrian court in exile. On that basis, as well as on the evidence of other records, a tradition has emerged assigning him the office of the queen's chancellor, though nobody can say for sure what that office involved. On the other hand, it does not seem too far-fetched to suspect him of a certain ambition to revive for himself the old office of first justiciar with all the duties incumbent upon it whenever the king was incapacitated (Richardson & Sayles, 1963:163-9). Such a position is more consistent with those subsequent activities by which he is remembered during the period of exile, such as the writing of disquisitions in favour of the Lancastrian dynastic legitimacy and against the Yorkist usurpation, and the instruction of the heir to the throne, Henry VI's only son, in the laws and the system of justice of his land, while also proferring him practical advice concerning the consolidation of the king's authority. Ten years later, when the Lancastrian crown prince Edward lost his life at the battle of Tewkesbury, on 4th May 1471, at which Fortescue, an old man by all standards, was present, he found himself in the position which he dreaded most, namely that of being at the mercy of Edward IV, the Yorkist usurper. His life was spared against all

odds and rumours to the contrary,and most likely not
because of his advanced age, but for more practical
reasons. His expertise in matters of government and
in the legal aspects of royal succession could have
been useful to the Yorkist monarchy in its own consolidation. On the other hand, the end of the Lancastrian king and his heir, through violent death, freed
Fortescue from allegiance to a virtually extinct royal
house. It also made it easy for him to acknowledge
the Yorkist monarch's authority. Nonetheless, if his
head was not chopped off at Tewkesbury, immeditately
after the battle, he was put in jail for a while,
and then banned to Ebrington, in Gloucestershire,
where he was kept under house arrest at his former
estate. Round 13th October, in the same year, he was
granted a general pardon for all his past offences,
and soon afterwards, was appointed member of the
King's Council. Nevertheless, the reply to his petition for reversal of attainder, by which he was re-
claiming his confiscated property, seems to have
been made conditional on another gesture on his
part, namely a public recantation of his earlier
writings favouring the Lancastrian legitimacy against
the Yorkist usurpation. He obliged in a way that was
not without dignity, or rather, in a way that turned
the lawyer's astuteness into the tool of dignity.
Known under the title of DECLARATION UPON CERTAIN
WRITINGS (1471-73), Fortescue's recantation of his
opinions admits imperfect knowledge of the Yorkist
pedigree as the cause that had led him to question
the dynastic claim of Richard, Duke of York, and
subsequently, of his son, Edward IV. The error was
amended as soon as the missing information became
available. Moreover, true to his profession and to
precedent, Fortescue played down his own ability as
common lawyer and former judge to provide a legal
solution to the succession question. Besides, the
fact that he had not attended any of the universities
stood him in good stead: he invoked it as an argument

in favour of his alleged ignorance and lack of speculative skills. Although a member of the King's
Council and eventually reinstated in his own livelihood, it is probable that Fortescue's public career
came to a halt after that. The date of his death is
as wrapped in mystery as is that of his birth, though
some scholars tend to push it beyond 1478.

*

It is as impossible to date with any degree of
accuracy the compilation of his treatise on government. His previous major work, DE LAUDIBUS LEGUM
ANGLIAE was, according to Chrimes (1942:lxxxviii),
completed before 1471. Given the fact that he arrived at Weymouth on 14th April (Plummer:1885:70),
one is left to presume that the later work was fin-
ished after his capture at the battle of Tewkesbury,
in which his pupil, Prince Edward, lost his life
(4th May) and before October of the same year, when
a general pardon for all past offences was granted
to him by Edward IV. It is very unlikely that he was
allowed to keep personal papers and books with him,
after his capture, and so one may be justified to
suspect that the English text, which ultimately survived in copies by various hands, was compiled from
memory, at Ebrington, during the house arrest.
Plummer's discovery of the "Seven Articles", reproduced in a modernized version as Appendix I of this
edition, shows that Fortescue had been at work on
the subject-matter of the treatise for some time before his return from the exile in France. Some of
its ideas had already been formulated in DE LAUDIBUS,
and might have been expounded verbally to his pupil
by way of an explanation of his own exile at St.
Mihiel in the Duchy of Bar, and to kindle in him the
desire to return to England and avoid his father's
mistakes. The precipitating factor, though, might
have been the negotiations with Louis XI, for whom
Fortescue wrote political memoranda on the situation

xiii

in England, on the one side, and the Earl of Warwick,
on the other, prior to the latter's return there.
Moreover, the fact that the surviving texts, both of
the "Articles" and of the treatise, are in English
points to two things: one that they were written in
haste and with a sense of urgency, and the other,
that they were meant for the ears and the eyes of
English monarchs, Henry VI and Edward IV, respectively, and their closest advisers. For diplomatic
reasons, Fortescue attributed the "Articles" to his
pupil and prospective king. Altogether different
circumstances rendered such a disguise redundant:
the treatise was to prove his own usefulness to the
Yorkist crown, after a life-time in Lancastrian
service. He seems to have pleased his new master as
he was able to legitimate the king's monopoly of
patronage, the basis of any centralized, absolute
monarchy.

*

Fortescue's treatise on government is neither a
a compendium of actual statues or formalized decisions of past councils and parliaments, nor a set of
rules defining two types of monarchy: the absolute
and the limited.Hence it is a disappointment for the
legal historian, as well as for the historian of the
period who would complain of the obsolete character
of its contents and the scarcity of factual detail.
It is for the social scientist that it makes fasci-
nating reading, first and foremost owing to his approach to the realities under discussion: social,
psychological, economic and political, by turn. Its
end-result is a sample of political history in the
making, a testimony of the changing course of a
particular type of society and the shifts it incurred
in its ideological make-up. It should be remembered
throughout that Fortescue was a civil lawyer, engaged
in property transactions, and a judge in the service
of the crown, who had been expected to issue opinions

xiv

on moot points of the law, besides writing into law
new bills passed by parliament. Another thing that
needs to be borne in mind throughout is the fact that
in the society in which Fortescue lived, politics
were practised characteristically, though not exclusively, through petitioning and adjudication of the
merits of the claims submitted in that way. As a
result, politics by and large assumed a legalistic
form.
Against this backdrop, Fortescue's major contribution is to political theory, through his concept of
royal and political dominion, resumed and expounded
in the treatise on government, that sets him firmly
among the precursors of the theoreticians of the modern state. Indeed, he made use of "old", canonical
terms, but it is the way in which he combined them
and the meanings which he instilled into them,
that one needs to pay attention to.
"Royal dominion" and "political dominion",derivative
from Aristotle's concepts of monarchy and politeuma,
respectively, had been assimilated into the body of
canon law, the law of God,the authority of which was
at the time still above anyone, kings included. They
are distinct, or rather one may say, opposite, concepts, to the extent they refer to one-man government
and government by a civic body or collective, respectively. To bring them together, Fortescue introduced
a middle term, so to speak, the concept of "common
good", that through Aquinas had also been included
in canon law. By making out of this concept the
shared purpose of his political power structure,
Fortescue brought the monarch and the commons, the
polity, together, as subservient to it. Their respon-
sibilities, social and political, too are defined by
this purpose, as a consequence.
Fortescue called it by turn "public" or "universal",
though, and I suspect that he did it deliberately,
in order to avoid a possible misunderstanding by association, through a literal translation of Aquinas'

bonum commune by "the good of the commons", that is
the good of a particular social category of free
people with a certain income of their own, to which
Fortescue himself belonged. Nonetheless, the terms
"public good" had been in circulation in England for
some time, both within the civil law and outside,
so Fortescue cannot be ascribed authorship. His contribution lies in the weight and position which he
came to assign them within the political power
structure. What is this "public good" which looms so
large, first in the "Articles" and then in the
treatise itself?
The Thomist doctrine of the common good points to the
attainment of wordly happiness through temporal
welfare, which renders compatible the pursuit of a
superior, other-wordly end. Fortescue, however, interested as he was in the here and now, left out the
other-wordly aspect and concentrated on the temporal
welfare. Moreover, the use of "public good" instead
"common good" could better accommodate the distinction between the public and prive dimensions of the
lives and interests of those involved in its pursuit,
not least of them, the king's, who as Bracton remind-
ed everyone, was under the law. It is Fortescue's
main criticism of the magnates on the King's Council
that they only served their own interests at the
expense of the crown's and the country's. As its
scope coincided with that of the whole society,
public good was a resilient principle, which accom-
modated not only the community, but also the individualism of each member of the society, taken separate-
ly, and not excluding the penchant for lawlessness
and resistance to an authority that was not backed
by force.
By and large, Fortescue's insistence on this principle gives the reader a certain feeling of "déjà-vue".
The impression, although real enough, is actually
based on a misunderstanding:its association with the
lingering principle of the 19th-century liberalism

in its pursuit of the greatest happiness for the
greatest number. The feeling is reinforced to a degree by a shared emphasis on the economic aspect of
politics, unlike the Thomist concept, with the
latter's emphasis on peace through the administration of justice as the instrument of its achievement.
Material poverty, in Fortescue's opinion, bred lawlessness and disorder both in the crown and in the
common people. Consequently, and as a member of the
new gentry, he regarded it as natural that man
should aspire to better himself. Thus his concept
of public good addressed both the crown and the commons: it made mandatory for the former to become
effective in securing for each and everyone the conditions that would enable them, through their indus-
try, to lead a contented life within the community,
free of worries about the day after. The latter,
though, were obligated to support the crown in their
own interest, and against all the attempts to inter-
fere with the smooth course of this commerce, isolate
the crown and kidnap it, so to speak, in order to
make it serve the private interests of a handful
that were likely to fall foul of each other over the
booty.

*

Traditionally, royal authority had been conferred by
force. In other words, in order to make the barony
obey him, a king had first of all to win the trial
of arms over the other candidates, his peers. To put
it briefly, he had to conquer his territory. Later
on, other conditions were added regarding lineage
(direct royal descent), the consent of the people,
expressed through the clamour of the three estates,
the clergy, the barony, and the commons, and lastly,
the candidate's willingness to take and be guided
by the oath which he was expected to take at coronation.
In line with his notion of public good, Fortescue

focussed on the last aspects, those related to the
contents of the oath and its binding power. From the
royal oath in force since 1308, Fortescue took over
the king's obligation to preserve laws, customs and
liberties for his people and to fulfill his judicial
duties. Eventually, as protection of person and
property (the former being the main object of the
king's criminal justice, and the latter of his
civil justice), those obligations became the princi-
pal functions of Fortescue's royal and political
dominion, alongside the defence of the borders.
The royal sovereignty may be easily tracked down to
the office of supreme, inappelate judge that the
king was meant to be. Furthermore, Fortescue's task
to attribute sovereignty to the king had been made
easier by a decision of the King's Council of 13th
November 1437, recorded in the minutes of that day's
session and stating the formal abdication of its
corporate political power by the baronage in favour
of the king, while keeping for itself a consultative
and an executive role only, with discretionary powers
in routine matters alone whenever there was unani-
mous accord on those matters. Thus, theoretically
at least, Fortescue had no difficulty in subsuming
the baronage to the supreme purpose of the political
machine, the public good. Besides, England had been
a centralized monarchy for half a millenium already,
and so, as a principle, it raised no technical
problem when it was included in Fortescue's political
power system. On the other hand, Henry VI's long
minority and his subsequent spells of disability
made the notion of kingly office apart from the
person of any particular holder easier to grasp by
all and sundry. An old concept, that of the crown,
gained a new lease of life, in that way.
It raised the office above the holder who was made
its custodian, and so was placed under the obligation
of fulfilling its functions with a view to perpetua-
ting it as a guarantee of universal welfare. A

country-wide bureaucratic network in the pay and under the exclusive orders of the crown was to reach
out and incorporate all social groups, distributing
justice and administering the crown's patrimony,
which had to exceed that of the richest barons,
through the creation of a crown monopoly of inalienable imovable property. Money payments and perquisites were to be the tangible benefits for service
performed under oath within this bureaucracy. What
Fortescue promoted was authority validated by administrative efficiency, which in the conditions of
cash-nexus, not only needed extensive financing but
had to show profit continuously. To enhance it,
he separated the royal household and its management
from the crown as office, in keeping with the imper-
sonal character of the latter, and down-sized the
king's council of barons. He made good the reduction
by introducing a council of salaried experts with an
advisory role only, for the king's exclusive use,
enabling him to make informed decisions for the public good. The idea for the council of experts might
have come to Fortescue from his experience of the
baronial councils, made up of lawyers, attached to
the estates of the high barons, such as the Earl of
Warwick. He could have also drawn inspiration from
the workings of the parliament in Paris, that he had
been given the occasion to observe at close quarters.
Through its composition, the council of experts was
meant to secure the link between the commons and the
crown at the highest level, outside parliament
and to lend its weight in the formulation of royal
decisions. It provided a necessary screen between
the king and the claimants challenging his patrimony, and checks upon rash and unwarranted decisions
on the part of the monarch that would prejudice his
office.
By and large, Fortescue divided the polity into two
broad camps, the baronage and the commons, the
latter including everybody who was a free person

but not a baron. (Personally, he had little love to
spare on the baronage of his day, with its arrogance
and disruptive, self-serving patronage at the expense
of the crown, and a permanent threat to those not in
their service.) He was aware that the barons needed
the crown to the extent it could authoritatively
settle disputes in their ranks, keep in check the
aggressive and the rapacious, and punish those who
endangered the social order and the security of the
realm. He was equally aware of the fact that they
would refrain from effectively acknowledging the
authority of a king unable to exert patronage and
deliver the duties of his office, and so would
refuse to heed his royal summons. Common law, like
canon law earlier, as well as the traditional system
of general taxation had rendered the divide between
baronage and commons in England by far more surmount-
able both socially and economically than, say, on the
Continent. On the other hand, not few were those
commoners who eschewed knighthood, for instance, although they had enough wealth to qualify for it. They
were avoiding it because they were too wealthy
and so could do without the burden which the obligations of knighthood would have imposed upon them.
It was this new social category which had come to
prosperity and even wealth through managerial skills,
business acumen, commerce and profiteering, and even
legal practice, that Fortescue wanted to integrate
into his system of domination by allotting it a pro-
portionate share of responsibility, in parliament and
local administration, for the universal welfare.
The parliament was the only place where the monarch
could petition his subjects, through their representatives, by submitting his draft bills to it. As an
institution, it was the closest approximation of
Fortescue's idea of political dominion. What he
wanted of parliament, though, was not to allow it
to assert its will over that of the king, but rather,
to work for the redress of the authority of the crown

through a legislation that would redefine the dimensions of the crown patrimony in a way that would render onerous taxation redundant, without for that matter putting the realm at risk. The parliament was to protect the crown and its patrimony from any arbitrary alienation with negative consequences for the public good. At the same time, the crown was to be guaranteed enough material and financial resources that would give it a long-lasting economic advantage over parliament with its power to grant subsidies. As with the council of experts, the relation between the crown and parliament was meant to be consensual and legalistic, based on the economic principle of money for value. The commons would be induced to pay and support the crown only if given good service by it. Material self-interest is behind the consent in which Fortescue's royal and political dominion is grounded. The system, though, does not lack a certain resilience, resulting from this very interdependence, Expert counsel could compensate for a lack of personal talent in the holder of the kingly office, while the indecision and procrastination of parliament and royal councillors could be circumvented by a king exercising his sovereign power.

Fortescue did not favour the baronial solution of violent removal of inadequate performers of the royal office. As a man of law and order, he might have dreaded the unpredictability of its immediate consequences, but also the blow dealt to crown authority in that way, pivotal as it was to the political power structure devised by him. Such an act was negating the very concept of royal sovereignty. Legitimate continuity in the holding of the supreme office was thought by him desirable at all times: inadequate performers could be either isolated (but not formally incarcerated) or convinced to abdicate of their own free will, in favour of a legitimate heir, and then allowed to die a natural death, as the "Articles" allow one to surmise.

xxi

Much has been made of Fortescue's nationalism, so perhaps something should be said about it here, before concluding. In his IN PRAISE OF THE LAWS OF ENGLAND, probably compiled towards the end of his exile in France, Fortescue was trying to awaken the interest of his charge, the royal prince, in the country of his father, and in its institutions which were different from those of France, the homeland of his mother and of his grand-mother, on his father's side, but in which he had spent the best of his seventeen years, growing into an accomplished warrior. He was motivating the plans for the prince's return to England and preparing him for the office of king. Moreover, he could have found it hard to resist the temptation of praising a judicial system at the head of which he had once been, second only to the king. After all, it was his professional pride and competence that were at stake.

In the treatise ON GOVERNMENT, things are somewhat different, even if whole passages from the other work found their way in it. On the one hand, he tried to make out a case in favour of ethnographic, psychological, geographic, economic, historic and institutional differences among countries. On the other, he was exploiting a self-serving tactic: praising everything English to dispel suspicions about his French connections and at the same time to reaffirm his loyalty to his country. His Francophobia is less profound, though, than he let one think. If, as already said, the baron's council may be considered a model for his council of experts, he was confirmed in the practicality of his recommendation by the workings of the parliament in Paris, to which he would refer as an example. Moreover, French fiscal policies gave him ideas about potential sources of

revenue for the crown, while the inalienability of
French royal domains showed him not only the advantages which that principle represented for the crown
but also its feasibility.

Perhaps it would be more appropriate to talk not
so much of nationalism as of a patriotism tempered
by his experience as justice of peace and than
judge of the king, who had to struggle with the
anarchical individualism of his countrymen. It was
that which after all had brought about the crisis of
central authority, a victim of which he eventually
became. At the same time, he was aware of the need
to define the new situation created through the loss
of all the English possessions on the Continent, save
Calais, useful as it remained for a while to preserve
the image of the Channel as an English sea. The age
of insularity began in Fortescue's life-time, but
it would take longer to develop the feeling of its
consequent, the vulnerability of its shores and borders, throughout the country. Even longer time would
be needed to counterbalance it through policy.
Fortescue's insistence on the necessity of military
defence was the sound reaction of an insider obliged
to delve into foreign politics, while given a chance
to look at his country from the outside.

*

Sir John Fortescue was a lawyer, a civilian, to use
a term current in his time, who made his wealth from
property transactions. He became a magistrate and
eventually the highest judge in the most political
of the law courts, the King's Bench. His occupation
was the practice of law and the distribution of
justice according to the standards of the times, and
between them, the management of his own assets. He
had been sent to Lincoln's Inn to be trained in the
practicalities of the most lucrative, lay profession
of the age. He had not been trained in the theoreti-

cal and speculative thinking of the universities, and his admission of ignorance in the "Declaration" was not just diplomatic or hypocritical humble pie. One must always remember all this when considering his main writings, which after all, were addressing specific practical issues, and were put together in exile or under house arrest, with little if any source material at hand. Moreover, he compiled them in his old age, which is to say that he was already too inured in his ways of thinking as a practising civilian to be able to do the about-face and become a theoretician of the constitutional monarchy, as some modern scholars have expected him to have been. To reiterate, Fortescue happened to witness and experience directly and at his own expense some of the deterioration of that political structure that had kept his country together. It made itself manifest not only through violence, in virtue of the old Augustinian dictum, that in the absence of justice it is the robbers who have the field, but even more in the anomalous situation of the simultaneous presence of two kings, albeit one of them in protective custody, for the most part of a decade. The shrinking of the borders to the insularity of the British isles, which gave everybody but the coastal fishermen a feeling of safety, added to the general indifference to matters of foreign relations and overall defence. Kingship tended increasingly to be regarded as redundant, an evil from which one should stay away for better or for worse, as long as it was unable to protect persons and their property.

It was in such circumstances that Fortescue concentrated and insisted upon sovereignty within the political entity of a country, or of the polity, as sometimes he himself would call it. He went on to reassess the overall importance of kingship in society by making it the condition sine qua non of the survival of the nation as a coherent entity, capable of reproduction. To the lords' redefinition

of the royal sovereignty in the first half of the
15th century, he added his personal conviction that
decision-making was a one-man action in matters of
urgency and wide scope, affecting the many in more
than one way in the long run. His experience as
chief justice had led him to that conviction. The
context allowed him to differentiate between force
and authority, yet both necessary, if the person
at the apex of a centralized system of government
was to function satisfactorily and follow through his
decisions. Sheer force, a monopoly of violent means
arbitrarily employed, could not in the long run secure the survival of the society upon which it was
exerted. On the other hand, authority was in itself
a composite factor that did not exclude personal
qualities such as competence, consistency of judgment
and conduct, a sense of reality and timing, foresight
and good management, kept alert by a sense of mission
regarding the public good. Fortescue was convinced
that as such it was likely to attract force that
would place itself at its service either for the
leadership that authority provided or the material
compensation, or both. The offices which he had been
holding led Fortescue to think that real authority
did not shun force, but rather employed it judicious-
ly to consolidate itself. Together, as power, they
would secure the broadest range of consent within
his system of domination, the royal and political
dominion.

The consensual relationship was a give-and-take
relationship, whether formalized by contract or sanc-
tioned by tradition. The whole political power
structure was put in jeopardy whenever the formal
aspects of the domination relationship were suspended, regardless of the personal qualities of the
agents. The professional man of law (and order),
Fortescue never tired of driving this point home, and
by doing so, he legitimized the bureaucratic, secular
structure of the modern state in which the warring

lord had become redundant.

ON GOVERNMENT was written in the form of a baronial
counsel's argument about the recovery, preservation
and expansion of his lord's estate, with recommendations that at first sight have nothing new about them:
most of them had been circulated on occasion in the
first half of the century, some based on acts of parliament, while others as part of an even older tradition in process of overhauling. Nonetheless, it is
more than a compendium of technical advice, or
rather something else, besides, because the practicality of its recommendations remained a moot point.
Deliberately or not, through his combinations of no-
tions and redefinition of terms, Fortescue produced
an ideological platform, the legitimizing basis for
the new political power system which was taking shape
in England at the time, and which is now known as the
absolute monarchy. Proof is the popularity it gained
into the following century and beyond, until the precarious balance between the crown and the commons in
parliament tipped over in favour of the latter.

By his open displeasure with the high nobles and the
courtiers, and his emphasis on the increasing importance of the commons in the social and political
life of the realm, by lending new weight to the age-
old centralized monarchy, an institution peculiar to
his country, he redefined sovereignty before Bodin,
and anticipated Machiavelli with his concept of the
state. In the process, he came to point to the major
peculiarity of the English absolute monarchy, namely
the higher proportion of consent that went into its
domination relationship, based on value for service
or the contractual principle.

SIMONA DRAGHICI

xxvi

CHAPTER ONE

THE DIFFERENCE BETWEEN ROYAL DOMINION[1] AND ROYAL AND POLITICAL DOMINION[2]

There are two kinds of kingdoms, one of which is a lordship called royal dominion,[3] and the other, royal and political dominion.[4] The difference between them lies in the fact that in the former, the king may rule his people by laws that he himself makes, and so he may impose taxes and other duties on them as he wishes, without their assent. In the latter kind of realm, the king may not rule his people by such laws that they have not consented to. As a result, he may impose no duty[5] on them, without their assent. This difference is clearly taught by Saint Thomas in the book which he wrote for the King of Cyprus, DE REGIMINE PRINCIPUM.[6] Nonetheless, it is more explicitly treated in a book called SUMMARY OF MORAL PHILOSOPHY,[7] and also, to a certain extent, by Giles in THE PRINCE'S GOVERNANCE.[8] Saint Thomas says that after God had chosen the children of Israel as his special people and ruled them sacerdotically,[9] he ruled them royally and politically[10] under the Judges until the time when they wanted to have a king, as did all the gentiles in those days, whom we call pagans, and who had no king over them but a man that ruled them royally.[11] God was greatly offended by their desire, their folly, as well as by their ingratitude, because they had already had a king who was God, reigning over them both royally and politically. Notwithstanding, they would exchange him for a king, a very man, that would reign over them only royally. Therefore, God threatened them, frightening them with thunders and other fearful things from heaven. And when they would still not give up their foolish desire, he charged the Prophet Samuel to declare unto them the law of such a king as they had asked for. Among other things, that king would take from them their land and goods, and give them to his servants, and load their children in his carts, and render them further harm,[12] as mentioned in the Eighth Chapter of the First Book of Kings.[13] Whereas beforehand, while they had been ruled by God royally and politically under the Judges, it had been unlawful for any man to take any of their assets from them, or hurt their children, without their being guilty of any offence. Whereby, it may appear that in those days a regime that was both royal and political,[14] was different from a regime which was royal only,[15] and that it was better for the people to be ruled royally and politically at the same time, than to be ruled only royally. In his book mentioned above, St. Thomas too praises the royal and political dominion,[16] because the prince that rules by such principles may not easily fall into tyranny as may the prince that rules just royally.[17] Yet they both are equal in estate and power, as it may easily be shown and proved by infallible reasons.[18]

CHAPTER TWO

WHY ONE KING RULES ROYALLY[1] AND ANOTHER RULES ROYALLY AND POLITICALLY[2]

Some people may wonder why one realm is a royal lordship only, and its prince rules it by his own law, called royal law,[3] and another is a royal and political lordship, and its prince rules it by a law called royal and political law,[4] when these two princes are of equal status.[5] The puzzle may be answered as follows: the cause of the difference lies in the original foundation upon which the two realms have been erected.[6] When Nimrod[7] set up the first realm by force and for his own glory, and subdued it

to himself by tyranny, he would not have it governed
by any other rule or law, but his own will.[8] Therefore, despite the fact that he had set up a realm
for himself, Holy Writ disdained to call him a king,
just because whoever reigns is said to be a king,[9]
which he did not, but oppressed the people by his
might and so was a tyrant, and was called the first
of the tyrants.[10] But Holy Writ calls him the mighty
hunter before God.[11] As the hunter takes the wild
beast to slay and eat it, so Nimrod subdued the
people to himself by means of force, in order to
seize their possessions, and turn them into his
servants, exerting upon them the lordship that is
called royal dominion alone.[12] After him, Belus, who
was the first to be called a king, and after him,
his son Ninus,[13] and later, other pagans, who followed
the example set by Nimrod in his realm, would not
rule by any other law but their own will. The laws
have been quite good under good princes, and better
than most, their kingdoms resemble the kingdom of God
who reigns over man, ruling him by His own will.[14]
Thus many Christian princes have used the same law,
hence it is said about the law that what pleased the
prince had the power of law.[15] So, I suppose, the
royal dominion first began in any realm. But afterwards, when mankind grew tamer and better disposed
to virtue, large communities, such as the companion-
ship that came with Brutus to this land,[16] wishing to
become one and turn into a body politic to be called
a realm, with a head to govern it - as the philosopher's saying goes: every community made of many
parts needs to have a head[17] - then they chose the
same Brutus to be their head and king. Upon their
settlement, organization and union into a kingdom,
they and he ordained that the realm be ruled and
justified by such laws as they would all assent to.
Hence their law is called political,[18] and it is also
called royal,[19] because it is administered by a king.[20]
The king of the Scotts reigns over his people by

this law, that is to say, he rules royally and politically.[21] As Diodorus Siculus says in his book,[22]
the kingdom of Egypt is ruled by the same law,
and so its king does not change its laws without the
consent of his people. In like form, Diodorus Siculus
goes on to say, are ruled the kingdoms of Saba, in
Arabia Felix, and the land of Lybia, and also the
greater part of the kingdoms of Africa.[23] Diodorus
praises that kind of rule and lordship greatly
in his book: because it is good not only for the
prince, who thereby may administer justice more safely than by his own arbitrement, but also for his
people who in that way receive justice such as they
themselves desire.[24] Now it seems to me that it has
been shown clearly enough why one king rules over his
people only royally,[25] and another reigns both royally and politically[26]: the former kingdom was founded
by the might of the prince, whereas the latter was
set up through the desire and organization of the
prince's subjects.[27]

CHAPTER THREE

*HERE ARE SHOWN THE FRUITS OF ROYAL LAW[1]
AND THE FRUITS OF ROYAL AND POLITICAL
LAW[2]*

It so happens that the French king rules over his
people royally,[3] yet neither Saint Louis, sometime
king there,[4] nor any of his progenitors had laid
new taxes or other impositions upon the people of
that land without the assent of the three estates,
which, whenever assembled, are like the parliament
in England. This order was kept by many of his successors long afterwards, until the English made such
a war in France that the three estates did not dare
to assemble.[5] Then, because of it, and because of the

great material needs which the French king had while defending that country, he took upon himself to lay taxes and other impositions upon the commons without the assent of the three estates. Nonetheless, he would not lay any such charges upon the nobles for fear of rebellion.[6] Because the commons there, though they grumbled, did not rebel, or were slow to rebel, the French kings have yearly laid such charges upon them since then, and increased the imposts so much that the commons have been reduced to poverty and destroyed, as they are scarcely able to keep alive. They drink water, eat apples with brown bread made of rye, eat no meat, but maybe at times, a little lard or the offal or heads of beasts slaughtered for the nobles and merchants of the land. They wear no woollens, but at best, if anything, a poor coat under their outermost garment, made of great canvas, and call it a frock. Their hose is also made of canvas and does not run below the knee, where it is gartered, leaving the shin bare. Their wives and children go barefoot. There is no other way for them to live.[7] Nowadays, some, who used to pay a crown[8] to their lord for the tenement which they rent from him by the year, pay five crowns to the king over that crown. Thereby, they are constrained by necessity to scour, toil and grub the ground for their sustenance, and so their nature is wasted and their kind is brought to nought. They wax feeble and crooked, unable to fight or to defend their realm; nor do they have weapons, or money to buy them with.[9] Truly, they live in the direst misery and poverty, though they dwell in one of the most fertile realms of the world.[10] As a result, the French king has no men of his own realm able to defend it except his nobles who, having no such taxes to pay, have kept in good shape. That is why that king is compelled to man his armies and retinues for the defence of his land, with strangers such as Scotts, Spaniards, Aragonese, Swiss, and other nations, lest his enemies may overrun him.

He has no defence of his own, but his castles and
forts. So this is the fruit of his royal law.[11] Were
the realm of England, which is an island and so may
not easily get help from other lands,[12] under the rule
of such a law and such a prince, then it would fall
prey to all the other nations, which would conquer,
plunder and devour it, a fact well proved in the
times of the Britons, when the Scotts and the Picts
so beat and oppressed this land that the people
sought the help of the Romans to whom they had been
tributary. Then, when they could not be defended by
the latter, they sought the help of the Duke of
Brittany, which was called Little Britain, and decided to make his brother Constantine their king.[13]
So he was made king here and reigned many years, and
his children after him, and great Arthur was one of
their issue.[14] But blessed be God, this land is ruled
by a better law, and so its people are not in such
penury, nor are they harmed in their bodies. Rather
they have become wealthy and have got all the things
they need for their sustenance.[15] As a result, they
have grown hardy, and are able to withstand the
enemies of this realm and to defeat other kingdoms
that have done or would do them wrong. So this is the
fruit of the royal and political law[16] under which we
live. Thus I have shown some of the fruits of both
laws: "You shall know them by the fruits which they
bear."[17]

CHAPTER FOUR

HERE IS SHOWN HOW THE REVENUES
OF FRANCE HAVE BEEN INCREASED

As our king reigns over us by laws more benign and
favourable to us than the laws by which the French
king rules his people, it stands to reason that we
have been of better use and more profit to him than

are the subjects of the French king unto him. Although it does not seem so when considering the fact that in a year his subjects surrender to him more than we do to our sovereign lord in two years' time, and that they do it against their will. Nevertheless, when one takes into consideration the two functions of the king's office[1]: one, the defence of the realm by the sword against the external enemy, and the other, the protection of the people by means of justice against internal wrong-doers, as it is made evident in the First Book of Kings,[2] mentioned above, it becomes clear that the French king overlooks them, though he may keep peace between subject and subject,[3] because he oppresses them himself more than all the wrong-doers of the realm would have done, albeit without a king over them.[4] As it is a sin not to give meat, drink, clothing or other alms to the one who is in need, as will be declared on Doomsday, how greater a sin it is to take from the poor man his meat, his drink, his clothing and all that he needs, which is just what the French king does to many a thousand of his subjects, as it is openly stated! [5] Although coloured as royal justice, [6] it is nothing but tyranny. As St.Thomas says, whenever a king rules his realm only to his own profit, and not for the welfare of his subjects, he is a tyrant.[7] King Herod ruled over the Jews royally,[8] yet when he slew the children of Israel, he showed himself a tyrant,[9] although the laws were saying that the prince's desires had the force of law.[10] For that reason, Ahab, who reigned over the children of Israel by such law, and craved the vineyard of his subject Naboth, would not by virtue of that law take it from him, but offered him its worth.[11] For these words, said to the Prophet, "preach to him the law of the Lord"[12] mean but preach to him about the Lord's power. [13] Thus whenever such a king does anything against the law of God or against the law of nature,[14] he does wrong, notwithstanding the laws mentioned above. It is so, in this case, that the law of nature says that the king should do to his subjects that which he would have done unto himself, were he a subject.[15] It may not lead to his demise as it almost has, in the case of the commons in France. Thus, although the revenues of the French king may, by such means, be much larger than those which the king our sovereign gets from us, yet they are taken without profit, as the power of his realm has almost been destroyed in that way.[16] On that consideration, I would not think desirable that the king's revenues, derived from the realm, should be increased by any such means. Yet, of necessity, they must be greater than they have been lately.[17] Truly, they need always be quite large, because as long as the king is abundantly provided, his estate may be honourably preserved for many a right cause,[18] some of which will be recalled below.

CHAPTER FIVE

THE HARM THAT RESULTS FROM A KING'S POVERTY

Firstly, if a king is poor, he would of necessity cover his expenses, and buy all that is needed for his estate on credit and by borrowing.[1] As a result, his creditors will win of him the fourth or fifth penny of all that he spends.[2] So he will lose whenever he pays the fourth or the fifth penny of his revenues, and in consequence, grows ever poorer, as usury and new deals[3] increase the poverty of the borrower. His creditors will always groan about overdue payments, and accuse his highness of mismanagement and defaulting. Were he to repay in due time, he would need to borrow as much again as he had borrowed at first. By that time, he would have grown poorer to the amount of the fourth or the fifth part of his expenses, and so become poorer and poorer until he turns into the most destitute lord of his land. Because such a manner of borrowing renders the great lords poorer than their tenants.[4] It is a dishonour to the king and a debasement of his glory, though, most of all, it is detrimental to his own security.[5] His subjects will rather follow a lord that is rich and can pay their wages and expenses than their king who has nothing left in his purse.[6] If they must serve him, then they will have to do it at their own expense.[7] Likewise, if the king is poor, he will of necessity make his gifts and rewards in the form of assignments,[8] for which he will get few thanks. A poor man would rather have a hundred marks in hand than a hundred pounds in assignments which probably will cost him as much;[9] or he may get his grant, yet never receive the payment it meant. Often, for lack of money,[10] the king will be willing to give his land away to such as would have been even more willing to have a hundred pounds in hand rather than land worth forty pounds a year, and all that to the great decline of the king's revenues and the depopulation of his realm. But the greatest evil that could result from a king's penury is that he will be constrained by necessity to devise new and refined means of acquiring wealth, such as finding fault with some of his subjects that have been innocent, and more often still, with those wealthier, because they might pay better, or making a show of ruthlessness where favour ought to have been shown instead, and of favour there where severity should be shown in such matters as the perversion of justice and the disruption of the peace and quiet of the realm. Because, as the philosopher says in his Ethics, without money it is impossible to function properly.[11]

Now one need not describe other damages that may affect a kingdom as a consequence of its king's poverty, however great the numbers of those left unmentioned. Every wise man can see them clearly. Indeed, no realm may prosper or be worthy of its name under the dominion of a pauper king.

CHAPTER SIX

PROVISIONS CONCERNING THE KING'S ORDINARY EXPENSES

Because the king needs always to be rich, which means that he must not lack sufficient revenues for the yearly maintenance of his estate,[1] it behooves that we first make an estimate of what his yearly charges and expenses are likely to amount to. His revenues then need to be proportioned accordingly, on that basis. Yet they need to be larger than the charges, in anticipation of any emergency that may befall him and his kingdom. For St.Bernard says that if a man's expenses be equal to his assets, an unforeseen incident may ruin his estate.[2] The king's yearly expenses consist of ordinary charges, on the one hand, and of extraordinary charges, on the other.[3] His ordinary expenses may not be eschewed.[4] To that end, part of the property needs to be assigned for their payment;[5] that apportioned patrimony should in no way be put to other use. If it happens that any grant is made of any part of that patrimony for any other use, then the patent bestowing it should be declared void and of no effect. If this principle were well established, the king's ordinary charges would always be paid in ready money, and the provision for them, always made in season.That would earn the king the fourth or the fifth part of the total of his expenses for ordinary charges.[6] This would in no way limit the king's power; for power does not lie in alienating and giving away more, but rather in accumulating more wealth and keeping it to oneself.[7] There is no power in committing sin, doing evil, or in falling ill, growing old, or in hurting oneself. All these states are the result of impotence. There-

fore, they may be properly called non-powers. That
is why the Holy Spirit and the angels, because they
may not sin, grow old, be sick, or hurt themselves,
have more power than we who can harm ourselves with
all these failures. So, whenever he does not do away
with the possessions necessary for his own sustenance, the king's power is greater than whenever he
deprives himself of them and alienates them to his
own hurt and harm.[8] Nor is this against the king's own
prerogative, by which he is exalted above his subjects. Rather, this is a prerogative to him, for no
man but the king may repossess the land that he had
once alientated.[9] The property allocated for ordinary
expenses should never be demanded from the king
afterwards, nor for that reason should his highness
think that he has got more assets to give away. With
that in view, he should all the more limit the number
of gifts made of other assets of his, as he might
consider them of no importance, because he will have
more need of them than those asking for them.[10]
The ordinary expenses, which the present author can
remember at this time, are the following: the king's
household and his wardrobe.[11] It so happens that the
king may wish now, or hereafter, to make his household less numerous than it was customary. Yet his
highness should have as many or more lords, knights
and squires, and others about his person than it was
customary, for his own honour and security, at his
expense, though perhaps no more than it was customarily costing him when the household was well man-
aged.[12] Thus one need not consider or purvey but only
for the king's house, which he may take over as such
or change in a new manner of his own, or still, in
any other form, at his pleasure, and as it would be
thought most expedient in keeping with the seasons.[13]
The expenses of the household may be estimated without delay by the older household officers and by the
clerks of the exchequer.[14] The second ordinary expense are the wages and fees of the king's great

11

officers, his courts of justice, and his council.[15]
This charge will always be considerable, and the officers in question must always be paid promptly. To have paupers in the house is not only unworthy, but it may also do the greatest harm that may befall any estate of the land, beside the king's. The third ordinary expense is the keeping of the marches.[16] Our yearly expenditure to that purpose is much higher than the Scotts'. Often we pay for the favours which we bestow upon the people who defend the marches, whereas the Scotts do not do that![17] The fourth ordinary expense is the keeping of Calais, which is a charge well known, indeed.[18] The fifth ordinary expenditure covers the king's works: what it amounts to yearly may not be ascertained. Still, the accounts kept by the clerks of the works will give an approximation, provided the king does not have his mind set on new works.[19] The defence at sea I do not reckon among the ordinary expenses. How much it would amount to yearly cannot be estimated. For it, the king uses the subsidy levied from tonnage and poundage.[20] Nor is that lesser reason why tonnage and poundage should not be considered part of the revenue which the king has for the maintenance of his estate, because it ought to be applied only towards the defence at sea. Although we have not always war at sea, yet of necessity, the king will always have some fleet at sea, in order to repress rovers, protect our merchants, our fishers, and the dwellers along our shores. The king should always keep some great and mighty men-of-war ready to disrupt any army coming to attack him from the sea. Lest it would be too late to build such ships.[21] Without them, all the king's navy will not suffice to withstand carracks [22] and other large vessels, and even less, to break a mighty fleet, gathered for that purpose. By now, as I suppose, we shall have counted most of the king's ordinary expenses. Wherefore, next we shall consider his extraordinary expenses, and that also as far as it

is possible for us to go.

CHAPTER SEVEN

THE KING'S EXTRAORDINARY EXPENSES

The king's extraordinary expenses should be so irregular that nobody could know their extent for certain in advance. Nevertheless, one may estimate their upper limit, and in case that is exceeded for good reason, then the whole realm will and must bear the particular burden.[1] Among such extraordinary expenses, as the present writer can now recall, there are the following: firstly, the king will often send his ambassadors abroad to the Pope and to different kings, princes and nations, and also messengers to the general councils.[2] Those ambassadors, procurators and messengers need to be honourably accompanied and well apparelled, both for the prestige of the realm and for the benefit of the missions for which they are sent at the king's correspondingly high expense. The latter will vary with distance, the length of their sojourn and the duties undertaken in their travels. Likewise, the king will have to meet unspecified yearly expenses for the reception of legates and messengers sent by the Pope, and of ambassadors sent by kings and princes, and also by great communities beyond the sea.[3] They will put the king to great expense during their stay, and also at their departure when they must be given handsome gifts and rewards. The king's magnificence and liberality lie in that very thing, and it is also necessary for the prestige of his realm.[4] Likewise, it is no good that he should reward such as render, or will render him service, or please him in other ways, out of the revenues and the possessions of the crown, or out of the assets of his inheritance, because they may be much more necessary for the preservation of his estate.[5] Therefore, the king will have to make such rewards with money out of his coffers.[6] Some have received such generous rewards out of those coffers, that they could buy themselves land with them, if they wish to. In this way, the king's estate will always remain intact. Besides, his highness will receive more thanks from some of them for the cash than for a grant of land. Moreover, ready money is the most convenient reward to anyone who has not served long. This expense will always be high, and in some years a great lord's estate will not suffice to meet it, even if he were to sell a large part of it. Truly, whenever the king rewards his servants in this way, he shows great favour to the entire realm. Likewise, the king must amass such wealth[7] that will enable him to erect new buildings as he wishes, for his pleasure and splendour.[8] He may buy himself rich clothes and furs, besides those that customarily fall under the yearly charges handled by the wardrober,[9] precious stones, fine linen, chains, baldricks,[10] and other jewels and ornaments befitting his royalty. Often, his highness will buy rich hangings and other apparel for his houses; vessels, vestments and other ornaments for his chapel, and also expensive horses and traps, and incur such high and noble expenses as befits his royal majesty, which the present writer cannot recall in detail, now. Were a king not to do so, then he would not live up to his estate, but rather in worse misery and deeper subjection than a commoner. The king will often send his commissioners fully armed, and his judges, too, in order to repress and punish rioters and rebels.[11] At times, he will ride himself to those spots, accompanied by an armed train of persons. All that could be accomplished only at great cost, because no man is bound to serve the king in such situations, at his own expense.[12] Likewise, in case of a surprise attack from the sea, or of a land invasion, the king must encounter the attackers with a

matching or even a greater army. The costs involved
will be met out of his own coffers, as no instant
financial aid from his people can be obtained so
suddenly.[13] Otherwise, he will put his whole realm in
jeopardy. Here, now, we have counted a large part of
the king's extraordinary expenses, and before that,
a great many of his ordinary charges. The time has
come to show how the king is able to meet these two
kinds of expenditure.

CHAPTER EIGHT

IF THE KING'S PROPERTY IS INSUFFICIENT, HIS SUBJECTS OUGHT TO MAKE IT SUFFICIENT

It has been shown above how necessary it is to al-
locate sufficient property for the king's ordinary
expenses, and that the revenue in question should
serve that purpose only, and not be alienated eventually. That allocation may in no way prejudice the
king, if any part of it is left after the payment of
the ordinary expenses. The balance is the king's own
money which then he may put to other use, at his own
pleasure.[1] As there is now no doubt left that the
king must have enough property to be so allocated for
his ordinary charges,[2] it remains to examine the ad-
ditional revenue made available to the king to meet
his extraordinary expenses, and in case it is inadequate, the ways to make it adequate, because his
realm is bound by right to sustain him in everything
necessary to his office. As St.Thomas says, the king
is given for the sake of the kingdom, and not the
kingdom for the sake of the king.[3] Thus, all that he
does ought to be referred to his kingdom. Although
his status is the highest temporal estate on earth,
it is still an office in which he ministers the
defence and the justice of his realm.[4] So he may say

of his realm and of himself what the Pope says of himself and the church, when he writes "servant of the servants of God." [5] *For that reason, just as every servant ought to receive sustenance from him whom he serves, so ought the Pope to be sustained by the church and the king by his realm. Nobody serves in in the army at his own expense.* [6] *Our Lord says that it is honourable to work for one's keep.* [7] *Therefore, the apostle says: "When anyone is under instruction in the faith, he should give his teacher a share of all the good things he has."* [8] *Thus, as every kingdom is bound to sustain its king, how much more are we bound to our realm over which our king reigns by such favourable laws as mentioned earlier.*

CHAPTER NINE

THE DANGERS BY WHICH OVERMIGHTY SUBJECTS MAY THREATEN THE KING

As the extraordinary charges, mentioned above, are in such a state of flux that they cannot be assessed in advance, likewise, it is not possible to be precise about the revenues that will suffice to meet them every year. [1] *That is why, in this case, we need to use conjecture and imagination to think that there are not two lords in England, whose property suffices to meet the king's extraordinary charges. The king's revenues need to be above the part apportioned for his ordinary expenses, and also larger than the income of the two greatest lords in England.* [2] *Once enough income is apportioned and assigned for the king's ordinary charges, it may appear that various lords of England have more income of their own than is left in the king's hands for his extraordinary expenses. Such a situation would be not only embarrassing but outright dangerous to the king.* [3] *That is so because those lords, with more revenue on hand,*

16

do not bear the burden of such ordinary or extraordinary charges as the king, but only of their
households which are small by comparison to the
king's. In consequence, it would be necessary to secure a far larger income for the king than what he
has got already.[4] Man's courage is so noble that he
aspires naturally to high things and wishes to be
exalted, and as a result, forces himself to be ever
greater. About that the philosopher says: "I love
them all, but mostly those at the top."[5] Thus it has
often happened that a subject with as large income as
his prince's would not be slow in aspiring to the
estate of his prince, which he may easily take
over. On the likelihood that such a powerful subject
may assume the estate of their prince, the rest of
the subjects need to be under a prince twice as
powerful as their old prince. Such prospects enhance
any subject's desire to free himself from the obligation to contribute to his prince's sustenance, and
so be quite willing to support the wealthier man's
rebellion.[6] Indeed, such an enterprise is the more
feasable whenever the rebel has more wealth than his
sovereign lord. The people will go with the one who
would reward and look after them best. Such conduct
is known to have been practised in almost every
realm, and their chronicles are full of it. Ever
since it was inhabited by the French, there was never
a change of kings in the kingdom of France, but by
the rebellion of such mighty subjects.[7] Childeric,
king of France,[8] descended from Clovis who had been
the first Christian king of France,[9] was put down by
pippin, son of Charles Martel,[10] the mightiest subject that the realm of France had ever had until
then. Later, Charles,[11] descended from Charlemagne,
son of Pippin, just mentioned, by nine or ten gen-
eration, was chased from the kingdom of France by
Hugo Capet,[12] son of Hugo the Great, Count of Paris,
who was the most powerful subject of France, and as
a result, had been created and called Dux Franciae.[13]

In our days, we have seen a subject of the French king,[14] *so powerful that he challenged the same king and put him to flight, and afterwards besieged him in Paris, his greatest city, and so kept him there until the king conceded to his desires and to those of his adherents and agents. Lately, in our realm too, we have seen some of the king's subjects declaring war unto him because their revenues and offices were the greatest in the realm, otherwise they would not have dared to.*[15] *The earls of Leicester and Gloucester,*[16] *who were then the greatest lords of England, rose against their king, Henry III, and took him and his son prisoners in the field. Dreading such demeaning practice in his land, the late king of the Scotts banished Earl Douglas,*[17] *whose power and revenues were almost equal to his own. He had been moved to that act by no other cause but the dread of rebellion. The chronicles of every realm, and especially those of Spain and Denmark, are full of such examples, and so are the Books of Kings in the Holy Scripture.*[18] *Likewise, one cannot overlook the fact that, as a result of fresh disagreements at home, and also of marriages, purchases and other titles, the great lords of the land would often grow even greater than they are now, and some of them may become as rich and powerful as a king. That may be just as good for the country, as long as they do not aspire to a higher estate.*[19] *Such was the Duke of Lancaster*[20] *that waged war against one of the most powerful kings of Christendom, the king of Spain, in his own realm. All this is mentioned only with the intent to make clear how necessary it is that the king should own considerable possessions and patrimony of his own, for his own security, in case any of the lords happen to be excessively powerful, and so became a danger to his throne. Indeed, there may be no greater threat to a prince than a subject equal in power to himself.*[21]

CHAPTER TEN

HOW THE CROWN MAY BE ENDOWED BEST

Now that the likeness of the king's ordinary and extraordinary charges has been examined, and furthermore, it has been shown how necessary it is that he should have considerable property above those expenses, and greatly in excess of anyone else's in the land, an income which undoubtedly he does not enjoy at present, it behooves us to find out how the king may secure such an income. But first, the commodities it may best consist of. Sometime, the king of France had not as much income from domains, lordships and other private patrimonies as the king of England, as it appears from the fact that the Queen of France had to her dowry but five thousand marks a year, whereas the queen of England had ten thousand marks.[1] In those days, there was little more of the realm of France in the king's hands than the part called Isle de France. All the rest of the kingdom, such as Burgundy, Normandy, Guienne, Champagne, Languedoc and Flanders, with many other lordships, were in the hands of the twelve peers [2] and other princes and great lords. That is why the gabelle on salt and the quartage on wine were granted to the king by the three estates of France,[3] and that was no little subsidy. No man in France may eat salt, unless he buys it from the king, and it is now set to such a high price that the bushel, which the king buys for three or four pence, is sold for two shillings and a pence, and at other times, even more.[4] Besides, the fourth pipe of the wine made in France is no trifle either, because the cultivation of the grapevine is the largest commodity of the realm. But we do not have it in our land. Hence no such subsidy could be granted to our sovereign lord, except perhaps the tax on

19

the salt that comes hither,[5] in which case he would
have more grumbling than profit from his subjects.
In France, people salt but little meat, save their
bacon, and so they buy little salt, although they are
coerced to buy more salt than they would. Every year,
the king's officers bring as much salt to people's
houses as they reckon reasonable in keeping with the
number of men, women and children that dwell in them,
and they must pay for that amount, although they
would rather not have that much.[6] That rule would be
sorely abhorred in England, both by the merchants,
who are accustomed to be free to buy and sell salt
as they wish, and by the people who use it to salt
their meats more than the French do. As a result,
they would grumble about the king at every meal, for
treating them more severely than his predecessors.
Thus his highness would get from it as much as the
man who shore his hog: much cry and little wool[7].
The king of France collects certain taxes set by himself on every ox, sheep and other chattel that are
sold in Flanders and in other lordships of the Dukes
of Burgundy and downwards, and also on every jar of
wine, keg of beer and other victuals sold on his domains, and which is no little yearly revenue to him;
yet, he does it in spite of his people. God forbid that
our sovereign lord should do this to his own people,
without their grant or assent. Nonetheless, provided
that no better means of increasing the king's revenues could be found, such a subsidy should not
be deemed unreasonable, if the people consent to it.
As with the gabelle on salt, every man should bear
the charge equally.[8] If a better remedy could be devised, I do not think, however, that such a new
charge should be imposed on the people during the
reign of our sovereign king. His predecessors had
never thought of a charge like it. King Solomon
charged his people with heavier taxes than they had
been accustomed to bear, before his days. Then,
because his son, King Rehoboam, would not ease them,

the ten tribes, split into twelve parties, forsook
him and chose a new king for themselves, and never
afterwards were they his subjects again. Of that
desertion God himself said later: for this thing
is from me. [9] It is an instance which shows that it
is not to the king's profit to overtax his people. [10]
In consequence, I think that if the king could derive
the income necessary to maintain himself in office
from landed property in the form of lordships, manors,
fee farms, and the like, he would not be forced to
tax his people, but keep himself in their hearts
wholly, surpass in lordship all the lords of his
realm and allow none of them to grow as rich and
powerful, a thing which should be dreaded most in
all the world. In that way, within a few years, no
lordship would be left in the realm to give them the
edge. [11] Nor should they wax great by marriage, unless
the king so wishes, because it is to him that the
great marriages of the land rivert, and he may dispose of them as he likes. [12] Nor should any man receive
larger heritage by descent than the king, given the
fact that the greatest lords of the realm are all but
his cousins. Likewise, no man may come upon so much
land by escheat but the king, because no man has so
many tenants as he has. [13] Beside, no man may have the
escheat of treason but the king himself. Nor should
any man increase his revenue by purchase as much as
the king. [14] None of his tenants should alienate property without his licence, in which case he may prefer
himself. [15] Nor should any patrimony be kept as whole
as the king's, because he may not sell any of it
honestly, as others do. [16] Beside, any sale on his part
would be the hurt of all the realm, as was the sell-
ing of the castle and the lordship of Chirk, [17] which
was without precedent. God forbid that anyone should
see another like it. To sell a king's possessions is
properly called dilapidation of the crown, and therefore it is a great shame. Now we have found, indeed,
what kind of revenues are best for the endowment of

*the crown. But, as it was said before, the present
king has not enough of them in his possession, so it
is most convenient to go on and examine the ways by
which his highness may secure an income that should
be most adequate.*

CHAPTER ELEVEN

HOW THE KING'S PROPERTY, ALREADY GIVEN AWAY, MAY BE RECOVERED BEST

While *the holy patriarch Joseph governed the land
of Egypt, under the pharaoh, he ruled the people and
treated them in such a way that they consented to
pay, and paid the same king, the fifth part of their
harvests and crops, every year.[1] They still bear that
charge, and ever will. As a result, their prince,
who now is the Sultan of Babylon,[2] is one of the
mightiest princes of the world, yet the same Egyp-
tians have remained the wealthiest people under any
prince. From that we learn that it will be good not
only for our prince, but also for ourselves that he
should be endowed well. Otherwise, the patriarch would
not have made such a pact, in the first place.[3] In one
thing only, namely wine, does the French king take
more from his people than does the Sultan, since he
takes the fourth pence of it. Nonetheless, he takes
nothing of their grain, wool, or of any other staple
that grows on their land. At times, during his reign,
the king, our sovereign lord, had revenue from lordships, lands, tenements and rents amounting to almost
the value of the fifth part of the realm, not count-
ing the possessions of the church.[4] Had those sources
been still in his hands, his revenue might have been
larger than that of either of the two princes mentioned above, or of any king that reigns over Chris-
tians nowadays. But it is unlikely to happen, because
part of that property was returned to the heirs of*

those who had owned it some time earlier, some
of it by reason of entails,[5] some by reason of other
titles which the king considered and judged good and
reasonable. Some of the above-mentioned patrimony
has been given by his grace to such as served him
with distinction. As their fame would last for ever,
so it becomes the king's magnificence to make their
rewards everlasting in their heirs, to their perpetual honour and memory. Moreover, the king has given
part of his patrimony to his most worshipful brothers, who not only served him in the manner just
mentioned, but also are so near in blood to his
highness that it would not have become his magnificence to have done otherwise. Furthermore, some men,
who had done him service that was reasonable to be
rewarded, were given land by the king, for lack of
money. He has done the same by other men, regardless
of their merits, through the insistence of their
petitions. It is presumed that some of the latter
have received a hundred pounds worth of land, though
they would have been content with two hundred pounds
in hand. Thus, it is thought that if such gifts, as
well as those made regardless of merit, were revoked
and subsequently replaced by money, offices or other
grants for term of life, so that after the recipi-
ents' death, they would be returned to the crown, the
king would have that kind of revenue that would
suffice to maintain his estate.[6] If the revenue is
not that large, I hold it for certain that the people
of the land would be quite willing to grant him a
subsidy on such commodities of his realm as mentioned earlier.[7] It would make up for the deficiency in
his revenue. As a result, his highness will establish
that the same patrimony, as it is at the time, should
remain perpetually the crown's, without transferring
it to any other use. Otherwise, when that happens,
the commons will have to be charged with a new subsidy, and so would be kept always in poverty.

23

CHAPTER TWELVE

THE HARM WHICH WOULD BEFALL ENGLAND
IF THE COMMONS WERE POOR

Some people have said that it would be good for the king if the commons of England were reduced to poverty as are the commons of France. Then, they would not rebel as they do so often nowadays,[1] a thing which the commons of France do not do, nor could they, because they have neither weapons nor armour, nor any goods to buy them with. One may reply to this kind of people by quoting the words of the philosopher: those who have seen but few things will be quick with advice.[2] It is true that such people think little of the good of the realm of England, the power of which rests[3] with the archers who are not rich men.[4] Were they rendered even poorer, then they would not have with what to buy themselves bows, arrows, jacks or any other weapon of defence,[5] to enable them to resist the enemy, whenever he intends to attack us, which he may do from any and every side, given the fact that we are an island, and as already said, may not get help from any other realm soon enough. Thus we shall be a prey to all our enemies, unless we ourselves become powerful. That power rests mostly with our pecunious archers, and so they need not only to have such equipment, as just mentioned, but also to keep drilling, which may not be done on the cheap, as every expert fully knows. That is why the impoverishment of the commons, which means the pauperization of our archers, will be the destruction of most of the power of our realm. Likewise, if poor men do not rebel lightly, which is the opinion of those who for that reason would reduce the commons to poverty, how then could a powerful man that stirs up a rebellion be repressed when all the commons are so poor that they cannot fight and so are unable to help the king? Why does the king order the commons to be mustered every year, if it were thought good that they should have no weapon nor the ability to fight?[6] Oh, how unwise is the opinion of those men, because it cannot be backed up by any reason! Likewise, before, whenever the commons rebelled in this land, it was the poorest among them that were the greatest inciters and rebels. Thrifty men were reluctant to join in, fearing the loss of their possessions. Nevertheless, quite often, they went along being threatened with dispossession by those who were poorest. Hence, poverty seems to have been all the cause of such risings.[7] The indigent man is stirred to it by his poverty: he wants to get rich; and the rich go along, because they do not want to become poor, to have their possessions taken from them. What would then happen if all the commons were poor? Truly, this land would quite probably become like the kingdom of Bohemia, where because of poverty, the commons rose against the nobles, and decided that all their assets should be held in common.[8] It is the king's honour, and also his office, to make his realm rich.[9] It is his dishonour when he has but a poor realm, of which people would say that he reigns over beggars. Still, it would be even greater dishonour to render his realm poor after he had found it rich. Likewise, it would be against his conscience, if he were to take from them their assets without lawful cause, since the king ought to protect his people and their possessions.[10] God defend our king from that infamy, and give him the opportunity of augmenting his realm in wealth and prosperity, to his perpetual praise and honour. The realm of France never gives any subsidy to its prince freely, of its own good will, because the commons are so poor that they are unable to give anything of what they have. Their king, on the other hand, never asks any subsidy from his nobles, for fear that they would plot with the commons, and maybe overturn him. But our commons are rich, and so at times, they give to their king a fifteenth and a tenth, and often other large subsidies, as is his need, for the good of the realm and its defence.[11] Quite a large subsidy it was when the realm gave its king a fifteenth and a tenth of their revenues for the term of five years; and the ninth fleece of their wools and also the ninth sheaf of their grains, also for the term of five years.[12] This they might not have done had they been impoverished by their king, as are the commons in France. Neither has such a grant been made by any realm of Christendom, mentioned by any chronicle, nor is it likely, or has any reason to do so. They have not so much freedom as regards their possessions, nor are they subject to such favourable laws as we are, except in a few regions, mentioned above. Likewise, we see daily how people that have lost their assets and have fallen into poverty turn into thieves and robbers in no time. That would not have happened, had poverty not pushed them to it.[13] How many a thief would then be in this land, were all the commons poor! The fullest safety, truly, and also the greatest honour that may come to the king is that every estate of his realm should be rich. Because nothing may induce his people to rise but lack of assets or lack of justice. Yet, certainly, when they lack assets they would rise saying that they lack justice.[14] Nonetheless, they would never rise, were they not poor, but were the prince to abandon justice, then, indeed, he gives in to tyranny altogether.

CHAPTER THIRTEEN

ONLY LACK OF HEART AND COWARDICE KEEP THE FRENCH FROM RISING[1]

Poverty is not the reason why the commons of France

do not rise against their sovereign lord. In that land, there have never been people poorer than the commons of the county of Caux in our times.[2] It has turned almost into a desert for lack of tillers. The new husbandry practised there shows it quite well, by the way the trees, bushes and groves, grown while we were the lords of that county, are digged up and cut. Yet, astonishingly, the commons of Caux went up in arms and took our towns, castles and fortresses, and killed our captains and soldiers at a time when we had but few men-of-war lying nearby.[3] That proves poverty not to be what keeps the French from rising, but cowardice and lack of heart and of courage; no Frenchman has as much courage as the Englishman.[4] Quite often, in England, three or four paupers turned thieves would set upon six or seven God-fearing men and rob them all. But their like have not been seen in France where six or seven thieves have a hard time robbing three or four God-fearing men. Hence, it is quite seldom that Frenchmen are hanged for robbery as they have no heart to do such a terrible thing. Thus, in any year, there have been more men hanged in England for robbery and manslaughter than there have been for like cause in France, in seven years' time.[5] Likewise, no man has been hanged in Scotland for robbery in as many years. However, they have often been hanged for larceny, and theft of goods in the absence of the rightful owner. They do not have the heart to take a man's possessions while he is present and will defend them, which manner of taking is called robbery. But the Englishman's is a different sort of courage. If he is poor and sees another man with riches that may be taken from him by force, he will not spare the rich man, though he would the right-true pauper. Thus, it is not poverty but lack of heart and cowardice that keep the French from rebelling.

CHAPTER FOURTEEN

THE NEED OF RESUMPTIONS AND OF MATERIAL GRANTS TO THE KING

The review made above to give a clear idea of the harm which the poverty of the commons would cause to the king and his realm has been a digression from the matter in hand, namely the examination of the best ways of enabling the king to secure sufficient and long-lasting property for the maintenance of his estate. Therefore, it behooves us now to return to the point where we left and which, as I remember, was this: we came to the conclusion that it was necessary that all such gifts as have been made out of the king's revenues inconsiderately, that is to say, undeservedly or regardless of the merits of the recipient, should be rescinded, so that those who have rendered any service should not go unrewarded. It seems to me that this may not be accomplished satisfactorily without a general resumption, made by authority of the parliament.[1] Likewise, by the same authority, the king should be given a large subsidy, out of which his highness, with the advice of his council,[2] may reward the deserving.[3] In this way, he would not be obliged to reward them by parting with his own revenues, so necessary to maintain his estate. Nor should he reward those who need not have as much revenue as they have now, or so great an estate, considering that all such distribution of the king's patrimony is, as already shown, harmful to all his liegemen,[4] who because of it, will be coerced to pay a new charge for the sustenance of his estate. Still, as in the case of resumption, it is advisable that an honourable and notable council be established, by the counsel of which all new gifts and rewards may be moderated and made in such a way as never before.[5] It should always be provided that by reason of such resumptions no man should be harmed in the arrears of his property at the time, and those he will run after the resumption and before new gifts and rewards are granted him. When such a council is fully created and established, it will be appropriate that all supplications made to the king for any gift or reward should be sent to the same council, and there debated and deliberated: firstly, whether the supplicant deserves such a reward as he asks for. If he does, it still needs to be decided whether the king should give such a reward out of his own patrimony, while saving enough for the maintenance of his estate. Otherwise, such distribution would be no virtue, but a kind of prodigality, and as much, a dilapidation of his crown. Hence no private person will reduce his own patrimony by reason of liberality or reward so much that he may no longer keep the estate he had before. Truly, it would be better if a private person would go without the reward, which he well deserves, than by the reward that he receives, he harms the public good and the whole country. Thus, in order to avoid these two evils, the council may advise how such a person may be rewarded with office, money, marriage, franchises, privileges or other means of the kind, which the crown has got in abundance.[6] Indeed, were this order observed, the king would not be grieved by importunity of suitors, nor would the latter obtain the satisfaction of any unreasonable desire by importunity or brokerage.[7] Oh, what peace would accrue to the king by this order, and in what tranquillity would then his people live, having not the faintest discontent against those who happen to be about his person, as they use to have because of the distribution of his land, and also because of their ill-advice in many other matters; nor grumbling about the king himself, for the misrule of the realm! Every difficult case may be defined within this council, or the king may take any decision in *it. As the sage would say: there is safety there where there is much counsel.*[8] *Indeed, such continual council may well be called "much counsel",*[9] *because it counsels each and every day.*[10]

CHAPTER FIFTEEN

HOW THE KING'S COUNCIL MAY BE CHOSEN AND ESTABLISHED

The king's council used to be made of great princes and of the greatest lords of the land, both spiritual and temporal, and also of men that enjoyed high office and authority.[1] *Those lords and officers had almost as many matters of their own to deal with in the council, as the king had. Hence, whenever they came together, they were so preoccupied with their own problems and those of their kin, servants and tenants, that they attended but little, if at all, to the king's matters. Actually, there were few things that concerned the king alone, since most of them also touched the above-mentioned councillors, their cousins, servants, tenants or others to whom they owed favours. What lower man, sitting on the council, did dare to say anything against the opinion of any of the great lords? Why then would not some of the servants and advisers of the great lords induce the lords to partiality and render them as favourable and partial as the interested parties themselves? Then, no matter dealt with in council could be kept secret.*[2] *Often, the lords would tell their own advisers and servants who had sued them for those matters, and also who had been in their favour and who, against. How could such great lords counsel the king to refrain from giving away to other men's servants his land, offices, corodies and pensions of abbeys,*[3] *when what they desire most are such gifts for themselves and their servants? With that in mind, and taking into consideration other things to be mentioned later, it would be more effective that the king should have a council chosen and established in the following form, or in some other similar form. In the first place, twelve spiritual and twelve temporal men should be chosen from among the wisest and best disposed people that can be found in all the parties of this land.[4] They should be sworn to counsel the king, in a way devised to that end.[5] Above all, they shall accept neither fee, livery, nor rewards from anyone but the king. When they take their offices, they should be sworn in like the justices of the king's bench and of the court of common pleas.[6] These twenty-four should be permanent councillors, unless found wanting, or it pleases the king to change any of them at the advice of the majority of the councillors.[7] Every year, four lords spiritual and four lords temporal should be chosen by the king to the council for one year, in the same manner as the twenty-four mentioned above.[8] They all should have a head or a chief to rule the council, to be selected by the king from among the twenty-four permanent councillors. He will hold his office at the king's pleasure, and may be given the name of chief councillor.[9] The twelve spiritual members of this council need not be paid wages as big as the twelve temporal councillors, because they do not keep a household of their own in their counties while not there, as the temporal members need to do mostly for their wives and children. It is for that reason that the spiritual judges in the court of the parliament in Paris take but two hundred francs a year, whereas the temporal judges take each three hundred francs a year.[10] Likewise, the eight lords, who in virtue of their baronies and estates are the king's natural councillors[11] and so ought to counsel him at all the times the king so wishes, need not be paid large wages for their attendance at the sessions*

31

of the council, which is only for one year. After
all, temporal men, who by reason of their inheritance and property, are made sheriffs for one year,
take little or next to nothing from the king for
the service they render during that year.[12]   Although the wages of the twenty-four councillors may
seem a new and heavy charge to the king, yet when
considering the large wages that the great lords and
others who were of the king's council took for their
attendance in the past, they will no longer appear
so great a burden. The council of yore was in no way
so accountable to the king and his realm as this will
be.[13] Moreover, those wages will cease to be paid. I
can easily imagine that certain kings might have
given to one man, who had served them, as much property in a year as the wages of the twenty-four councillors would have come to. If the new wages are
thought to be a great burden to the king, the number
of the councillors may be reduced to, say, sixteen
permanent councillors chosen from among private
persons, with two spiritual and two temporal lords
to sit for one year. Then, they will be in all but
twenty people. Continuously and at such hours as
will be assigned, these councillors will assemble
and deliberate the difficult matters that have
chanced upon the king, and then matters of policy regarding the realm, such as the reduction of the out-
flow of currency, the increase in the inflow of bullion, and the recovery of plate, jewels and money
removed out of the country lately.[14] Truly intelligent
persons will not be slow in finding the right means.
Likewise, they will deliberate ways and means of
keeping high the price of merchandise produced in
this land and of increasing it, while lowering the
price of the merchandise brought into this country;[15]
of maintaining our navy and increasing the number of
ships,[16] and other such points of policy, to the
greatest profit and prosperity ever to come to this
land.[17] Likewise, the reform of the laws, in those

aspects that need amendment, should be discussed by
the council, with the result of expediting the work
of parliaments, which so will do in a month what they
would have done in a year, were the amendments not
debated by the council beforehand and submitted to
parliament in a ripe form for deliberation. [18] Whenever
they wish to, or their presence is desired by the
councillors, the great officers of the land, such as
the Chancellor, the Treasurer and the Lord Private Seal
may be part of the council. The Chancellor may act as
president, whenever present, and exercise supreme
rule over the council. Likewise, the judges, the
barons of the exchequer, the clerk of the rolls may
attend, as also all such lords whom the councillors
will desire to consult in difficult matters. It is only
when their presence is desired that they may attend,
but not otherwise. [19] All other matters of concern
to the council, such as the death of a councillor,
the election of a new one, the length of the daily
sessions, the time of recess, the length of permit-
ted absence of individual members and the formulation of the leave, and all the other articles necessary for the orderly functioning of the council
should be recorded by a lawyer [20] in a book to be
kept as a register or an ordinary, in the council
room, for procedural reference.

CHAPTER SIXTEEN

HOW THE ROMANS PROSPERED WHILE
THEY HAD A GREAT COUNCIL

As long as their council, called the Senate, was
great, the Romans became the masters of a large part
of the world, through the wisdom of that council.[1]
Afterwards, Julius, their first emperor,[2] counselled
by the same senate, won the monarchy of almost all
the world. By its means, too, Octavian, their second

emperor, ordered that all the world should be enrolled as subject to him. [3] But later on, when ill-
disposed emperors, such as Nero, Domitian and others,
slew a great many of the senators and held the counsel of the senate in contempt, [4] the estate of the
Romans and of their emperors began to decline and
has reached such a state of decay that nowadays the
emperor's patrimonies are no larger than those of
some of the kings that were subjects of the emperor
while the senate was still intact. [5] Such an example
may convince one to think that with a council like
the senate, the king will have a rich and prosperous
land as had the Romans, and besides, his power will
increase so much that he will be able to subdue his
enemies and all those whom he would care to reign
over. Many chronicles are full of such examples, and
in particular, the chronicles of the Lacedemonians
and of the Athenians, who while they prospered, had
the best advice and acted upon it more than any other
people in the world, except the Romans. But when they
scorned such counsel, they fell into abjection and
poverty, as the looks of the city of Athens attest:
it is now but a poor village, whereas in times past
it was the most impressive city of Greece. [6]

CHAPTER SEVENTEEN

SOME WARNINGS WITH REGARD TO THE
DISTRIBUTION OF THE KING'S OFFICES

If it pleases the king, he may grant office to none,
as long as he and his council are of the same mind. [1]
Otherwise, he should reward his servants with offices, and so there would hardly be any need to give
them rewards out of his own patrimony. Moreover,
offices should be given only to those who have served
the king. [2] In that way his power would increase, and
he would have his own body of officers, [3] ready to

answer his summons, whenever the king wishes to call them, and more reliable than the paid men that he has got now and who are in the service of the lords. The power of the country, second to the might of its great lords, lies mostly in the king's officers. They may administer those counties best where their offices are, which means every part of the land. A poor bailiff may do more in his bailiwick than any man of rank, dwelling within his jurisdiction.[4] Some forester of the king's, with no other income, may bring more men to the field in fine order for shooting than may some knight or squire with quite a large income, dwelling nearby but holding no office.[5] What then higher officers may achieve, such as the stewards of great lordships, receivers, constables of castles, master foresters and others, as well as justices of forests, justices and chamberlains of counties, the warden of ports, and their like! It is not easy to calculate the advantage which the king may derive from his officers, were every one of them to hold but one office and serve no other man but the king.[6] Nor is it easy to reckon how many men may be rewarded with offices, and to what extent, were they to be prudently granted. The king grants more than a thousand offices, besides those the holders of which I consider the king's officers, and which are given by my lord the prince.[7] Some of the latter may earn in office two hundred pounds a year, others, a hundred pounds, still others a hundred marks,[8] some may earn forty pounds, others fifty marks, and so downward. Thus, the smallest of them, though but a parker, taking two pence a day, still makes three pounds and ten pence in a year,[9] besides his dwelling in the lodge, his fuel, the cow for his milk and such other things, and the fees that come with his office. Hence his office is also profitable to him to the amount of a hundred shillings as fee or rent, which is a fair living for a yeoman.[10] How many men, then, of every estate and of every rank may the king

reward with offices and to what extent, without giving away his own patrimony! Truth to say, the patrimony of the greatest lord in England may not suffice
to reward as many men, although he would divide every
bit of it among his servants. Nor the two greatest
lords of England may compound so much power as the
king's, were his officers only and wholly his servants, and had every one of them but one office. Such
lords and other men that ask the king for offices
for their servants may argue that they and all their
servants will always serve the king, and that those
granted offices at their request will serve the king
better if they remain in their service, and that they
will help him and suffer none in their company but
who will do so.[11] One may answer to that, that it is
true that while in their company they would render
service to the king, but so they would have done even
without their ever being made the king's officers.[12]
Thus the king will not be served better by giving
offices to other people's servants, but rather worse,
as Our Lord says: "Nobody can serve two masters".[13]
The king will lose the offices, as no particular
service rendered him is linked to them, while the
officers in question would not think themselves bound
to the king for the offices granted to them by his
highness at the request of their masters, and not as
a reward for any service rendered or to be rendered
directly to the king. For that matter, their old
masters will be better served by them than they were
before, and as a result, their power in their counties will increase, whereas the king,[14] with fewer
officers, will be at a disadvantage to repress them
when they turn amiss. As a consequence, many a man
act such brokers and suitors before the king, intent
on winning his offices in their counties for themselves and their servants to such an extent that in
some counties no man dares to accept an office from
the king, without first securing the good will of
those brokers and engrossers of offices. Otherwise,

he would have no peace in his county, afterwards. Hence many serious troubles and quarrels have flared up in different parts of England.[15] With this in mind, it seems quite appropriate that no man should have any office from the king without first taking the oath to serve none other but the king, and not to accept any other man's fee and livery while he serves the king. Likewise, while in the king's service, no man should hold more than one office, except the king's brothers, who may hold two offices, or such men who serve the king about his person or in his council and who may have a parkership [16] in their counties, for their relaxation whenever they return home, or other similar office that they may hold through deputies. [17]

CHAPTER EIGHTEEN
HOW CORODIES AND PENSIONS
MAY BE GRANTED BEST

If it pleases the king, he may grant neither corody nor pension, of which he may dispose by right of his crown, of any abbey, priory, or other house founded upon hospitality by any of his ancestors, [1] before his intentions are conveyed to his council and decided together with it, and his highness becomes aware of its opinion in the matter. As a result, men of his household will be rewarded with corodies and enjoy honest subsistence in their old age when they are no longer able to serve. The clerks of his chapel, that are married or are not promoted, [2] should also be rewarded with pensions for their subsistence, without for that matter incurring any considerable loss of the king's revenues. That is so because such corodies and pensions had been originally given to the king for that same purpose. However, lately, other people than the king's servants would ask for *them, and by pressing with their petitions, have obtained a large number, to the king's great harm and the hurt of those servants, who for that reason, live in greater penury and without assurance of any subsistence in later times when they are no longer able to serve the king.*

CHAPTER NINETEEN

THE GREAT BENEFITS OF FIRM ENDOWMENT OF THE CROWN

When the king has recovered his revenue by the above-mentioned means or otherwise, then it may please his most noble grace to establish, and as it goes, to amortise the same patrimony to his crown, so that it may never be estranged without the assent of his parliament.[1] Then it would function like a new foundation of the crown, by means of which the king will become the greatest founder in the world. As other kings have founded bishopcrics, abbeys and other religious houses, the king will have founded a whole realm and endowed it with greater and better possessions than there ever was any realm in Christendom. This kind of foundation may not be against the king's prerogative, or his liberty, no more than is the foundation of an abbey from which he may take no part of the possessions he once gave it, without the assent of its assembly.[2] Nevertheless, this kind of endowment of the crown should be a greater prerogative to the king, because, in this way, he enriches his crown with such assets and possessions that no king may ever estrange in any part, without the assent of his whole realm.[3] Nor may this happen to the detriment of his prerogative or the power of his successors, because, as it has already been shown, it is no prerogative to lose any property, or to be able to waste it, or alienate it. All such things come from impotence, as does the ability to be sick or grow old.[4] Truly, if the king does so, he will bestow more alms daily in this way than will have been done by all the foundations that have ever been set up in England. Thanks to this foundation, every man in the land will be merrier every day, more secure, far better in body and in all his possessions, as every wise man may well agree.[5] The foundation of abbeys, hospitals and such other houses is nothing by comparison. It will be like a college in which all the men of England, spiritual and temporal, will sing and pray for it, incessantly. Alongside other anthems, their song will be: " Blessed be our lord God, for he has sent King Edward IV [6] to reign over us. He has done for us more than ever had, or might have had, any king of England before him. The harm caused while he was winning his realm be now by him turned into the good and profit of us all. We shall enjoy our own good more and live under justice, which we have not done for a long time, God knows. It is out of his charity that we have all this to enjoy in our own times." [7]

CHAPTER TWENTY

WARNING AGAINST PATENTS OF GIFTS

It is not to be understood from the premisses that without the assent of his parliament, the king should give land for term of life to men who have rendered him special services.[1] Thus the crown will not be deprived, because that land will soon return. Nevertheless, it would be appropriate not to give the same land again. [2] Otherwise, importune suitors will not mince their words about such reversions, and often ask the king to desist lest they are ruined. If that happens, the king may have no rest from such suitors until his highness gives again all the land that he once gave. So, he should use that land only for gifts, in the same way as offices, corodies and pensions.[3] Indeed, it would be quite appropriate that the patents for all the king's gifts should mention that they were passed with the advice of his council,[4] for term of a year or two. If such an order were observed, men would not be so hasty to ask for rewards, unless their merits are real, and many would then show more administrative proficiency, so that the king's council would deem them worthy of reward. On the other hand, those who do not obtain what they desire will have little reason to complain, considering that they have been turned down by the discretion of the king's council. Thus the king will have peace and quiet and be well protected against such insistent petitioners.[5] Still, he may overlook this order whenever it suits him.[6]

THE END

NOTES

Chapter 1

1.   ...dominium regale. Although he wrote his treatise in English, Fortescue rendered his concepts and technical terms in Latin, perhaps to lend them extra weight and make them sound more persuasive.

2.   ...dominium politicum et regale. The two categories of dominion had appeared in different contexts in his earlier major works: DE NATURA LEGIS NATURAE and DE LAUDIBUS LEGUM ANGLIAE, respectively.

3.   ... dominium regale.

4.   ...dominium politicum et regale.

5.   Meaning tax, imposition. It is worth noting that here Fortescue refers to fiscal policy and legislation only, thus warning his reader of the main topic of his treatise, from the very beginning.

6.   The reference is to St. Thomas Aquinas (1225-1274), the most important of the theologians of the Roman Church, and his book DE REGIMINE PRINCIPUM (The Rule of the Prince) which was a basic canonical authority on matters of government and public administration, although only partially written by him. More recent scholarship has concluded that only the first two books of the whole work are by Aquinas and that the rest is due to his continuator, Tolomeo of Lucca (d.1327). As a result, Aquinas' contribution is now known under the title of DE REGNO, AD REGEM CYPRI, while DE REGIMINE PRINCIPUM is left to cover Lucca's contribution. See Eschmann (1949: ix-x). This recent distinction is not observed here, as it complicates matters unnecessarily. Fortescue and his contemporaries were regarding it as one work, Aquina's, which is what matters in this context. The King of Cyprus to whom it was dedicated could have been either Hugh II of Lusignan (1253-1267) or Hugh III of Antioch (1267-1284), who succeeded each other as rulers of the Kingdom of Cyprus. See Eschmann (1949:xxx-xxxi). The

Latin title of the work is used throughout the present edition of Fortescue's treatise, in order to distinguish it from another writing, bearing the same title, but compiled by Aegidius Romanus. Fortescue repeatedly mentions St. Thomas Aquinas and his work in support of his own classification, rather than as a specific source of the latter. To strengthen one's argument by reference to a juridically accepted authority was a common lawyer's device, indirectly confirmed by Plummer's failure to find any line in Aquinas' treatise that would corroborate Fortescue's classification.See Plummer (1885:172).

7.   COMPENDIUM MORALIS PHILOSOPHIAE, the main work of Roger of Waltham (d.1336), canon of St.Paul, London, is a collection of disquisitions on the duties and virtues of princes, with historical illustrations. Fortescue mentions it in the same manner and for the same purpose as he does Aquinas' REGIMINE, without any specific reference to any part of its contents.

8.   DE REGIMINE PRINCIPUM. The actual name of its author, known as Giles of Rome or Aegidius Romanus, was Aegidius Colonna (1247?-1316). An Augustinian monk and disciple of Aquinas, professor of theology in Paris, tutor to the future king Philip IV of France, and archbishop of Bourges, Aegidius Romanus compiled his work as a manual for his pupil, the royal prince. Eventually, it turned into a very popular book, as the large number of its translations attests. Fortescue mentions it with the same purpose and in the same way as the other two authorities, without any particular reference to its contents.

9.   ...in populum peculiarem et regnum sacerdotale. The phrase is a combination of Deut. 14:2 and Exod. 19:6. DE REGIMINE repeatedly states that the Judges governed politically, while the Kings ruled royally. See DE REGIMINE II:8-9 in Luis Betino's modern Spanish edition (1931). The concept of political and royal dominion could be Fortescue's.

10.   ...regaliter et politice. Perhaps it should be underlined, unless it has already become clear, that by

"political" or "politically", for that matter, Fortescue means "collective" or "consensual" while referring to the way decisions are taken in certain groups of people or communities, and not to politics in the modern sense of the term.

11.   ...regaliter tantum.

12.   The Clermont edition reads:"also set their children in his works and labours and do to them such other many harmful things, as in..." (Works, vol.I, p. 449).

13.   See 1 Sam. 8:10-17.

14.   ...regimen politicum et regale.

15.   ...regimine tantum regale.

16.   ...dominium politicum et regale.

17.   ...regaliter tantum.

18.   See also DE LAUDIBUS, Ch.XI, 11, pp. 26-27 and 28-29 of the Chrimes edition with English translation, Cambridge, 1942. Here "estate" means status, the monarch's position within the social and the political systems. On the other hand, it is obvious that Fortescue draws a distinction between physical violence and power, regarding the latter as an attribute of kingship. His notion of power is a composite, consisting of authority and a monopoly of physical force that is instrumental in the enactment of the law, or as he prefers to say, of justice, which in its turn is a product of authority. Put more simply, it is force tempered by and serving the authority of the law, the ultimate purpose of which is the public good. The difference between the two kings is only secondary to their position, because it does not refer to their prerogative or sovereign power, but rather to preliminary phases of their decision-making: the latter tends to ground it on a broader consultative basis than the former. That basis, however, is no guaranty of the soundness of any particular decision. At most, it may reduce arbitrariness and resistance to it by access to broader and more diversified knowledge of the state of things within the scope under consideration,

and likely to be affected by a specific decision yet to
be taken.

Chapter 2

1. ...regaliter tantum.

2. ...politice et regaliter.

3. ...jus regale.

4. ...jus politicum et regale.

5. See also DE LAUDIBUS, Ch.IX, 11.15-25, loc. cit.,
pp. 24-25. Fortescue thus renders explicit the nature
of the difference between the two categories of monarchs,
which he simply stated at the end of the preceding
chapter. The difference lies in their respective legislation. See note 18 above.

6. Consistent with his institutional approach, Fortescue
tries to explain differences by the perpetuation of
original distinctions - topographic, social, economic
and psychological - through time.

7. All that is known about Nimrod may be found in Gen.
10:8-12, which combines two contradictory sources: one,
describing him as founder of kingdoms, and the other,
as a mighty hunter. The tradition, used by Fortescue,
that represents him as a conqueror and tyrant could not
be identified.

8. Actually, the sentence does not end so, but goes
on: "by which and for the accomplishment thereof he made
it." This has been edited out to avoid repetition. On
second thoughts, however, attention needs to be drawn
to Fortescue's insistence on the idea that Nimrod set up
a realm, a kingdom, as a vehicle for the accomplishment
of his own will. Thus Fortescue not only presents the
foundation of political communities as purposive action,
but also introduces the notion of the primacy of individual interest in the foundation of a structured community of people for the purpose of serving that individual interest alone. Later, he uses it as a contrasting notion which he opposes to the royal and political

dominion, the result of enhanced, collective, political consciousness, guided by the principle of universal good.

9. ...quia rex dicitur a regendo. This Latin paraphrase could have been coined by Fortescue himself. The idea behind it was the common stock of common law, as Plummer (1885:185) found out. It is possible that through Bracton it had entered the lore of the inns of court and also of the English common law. By rendering it in Latin, Fortescue uses it as an authority.

10. ...primus tirranorum.

11. ...robustus venatur coram Domino. See Gen. 10:9.

12. ...dominium regale tantum. See also DE NATURA, Ch.7, p.   , and DE LAUDIBUS, Ch.12, 11.17-23, loc. cit., pp. 28-29.

13. Belus and Ninus are also mentioned in DE NATURA and in DE LAUDIBUS. In the latter, Belus is said to have reduced the Assyrians to his behest, and Ninus, a great part of Asia. In DE NATURA, Fortescue gives St. Augustine's CITY OF GOD, 16:17, as his source; but see also 4:6, 16:3 and 18:2 of the same.

14. Here Fortescue introduces another category, namely that of charismatic dominion in which the legislation is divinely inspired, and consequently emulates the perfection of the heavenly kingdom. It is a kind of rule conditioned by the personal qualities of the ruler, and not by his monopoly of coercive power, even though the distribution of justice is still considered the essence of government.

15. ...quod principi placuit legis habet vigorem. Part of a sentence from Justinian's INSTITUTES 1;2:6, it is a favourite quotation of Fortescue's, repeated both in DE NATURA and DE LAUDIBUS. It is probable that Fortescue reproduced it either from Bracton (fo.107), Glanville (p.2 of the Hall edition) or any authority derived from them. In disagreement with Plummer (1885:185), who maintains that Fortescue uses the quotation to underline the very principle of autocracy, it appears quite clear that Fortescue associates the principle with that kind of

rule "under Christian princes," that is to say, inspired by the teachings of the faith which had the heavenly kingdom as their main focus and exemplar. After all, the quotation is employed to support his previous statement, in the same way as the other authorities are referred to.

16.   The mythological great-grandson of Aeneas, Brutus is presented as the eponymous founder of the nation of the Britons in HISTORIA REGUM BRITANNIAE by Geoffrey of Monmouth (1100?-1155). Fortescue's source may be Geoffrey of Monmouth's work itself (1:15-16), or a later book, DE MORALIS PRINCIPIS INSTITUTIONE by Vincent of Bauvais (1190-1264), known to have once been in the possession of Fortescue. See Plummer (1885:186).

17. The philosopher is Aristotle, and Fortescue's paraphrase refers to Aristotle's POLITICS 1:2:9. In this way Fortescue legitimizes monarchy by direct reference to Aristotle, who thanks largely to Aquinas, has been raised to the rank of authority in the canon law.

18.   ...politicum.

19.   ...regale.

20.   Here follows a rather fanciful etymological explanation in Latin of the term "polity", which reads: "Policia dicitur a poles, quod est plures, et ycos, scientia; quo regimen politicum dicitur regimen plurium scientia sive consilio ministratum." It may also be found in DE NATURA, 1:23. As such, it sounds like one of those definitions which students must have been obliged to learn by rote when they were taught Latin, and to a lesser extent, Greek. The following is a free translation:"Polity is derived from poles, which means plurality, and ycos, which means science, knowledge; whence by political regime it is to be understood a system of government administered by the advice of many." See also note 10 to Ch. 1, above, for the way in which Fortescue uses the term "political" in this treatise. On the other hand, the term "policy" raises no difficulty: it is still used in the way Fortescue employed it.

21.   ...regimine politico et regale. In principle,

he was advised by his great council, made up of tenants-
in-chief, who in certain cases could, and were, represented by commissaries.

22.   Diodorus Siculus, Greek historian, lived mostly in
Sicily, in the 1st century B.C. He is the author of a com-
prehensive BIBLIOTHECA HISTORICA, in three parts and
forty books, in which the mythological stands alongside
the historical, and which covers events ranging from
before the Trojan War and up to Caesar' Gallic War.
It is quite probable that Fortescue was familiar with
the Latin translation of the first five books, made
by Poggio Bracciolini (1380-1459), who himself visited
England between 1418 and 1422, under Bishop Beaufort's
patronage. John Skelton used Poggio's version for his
own English translation which he completed before 1490.
Fortescue has already referred to Diodorus Siculus in DE
LAUDIBUS, Ch.13, 11.17-31, loc. cit., pp.32-33.

23.   See BIBLIOTHECA HISTORICA, Book II.

24.   See BIBLIOTHECA HISTORICA, Book IV.

25.   ...dominio tantum regali.

26.   ...dominio politico et regali.

27.   The "message" of this chapter is that wherever
custom alone is no longer applicable, the prevision and
predictability of law, so necessary to the viability of
any organized community, can be secured only by consensual legislation, or at least, by that kind of legislation which takes into account and reflects the circumstances as they are. This idea will be restated throughout the treatise.

Chapter 3

1.   ...jus regale...

2.   ...jus politicum et regale.

3.   ...dominio regali.

4.   Louis IX (1214-1270), king of France, canonized in
1297, was the most popular of the Capetian monarchs.

Fortescue commits a historical error by attributing him parliamentary rule. Actually, Louis IX would ideally fit that category of Christian princes mentioned in the preceding chapter, and who by the laws they gave tried to emulate the kingdom of God.

5. The statement is historically incorrect, and the cause given by Fortescue is naïvely fictitious. The Estates General were called by John the Good (1319-1364), when the English invasion of France could not be halted for lack of funds. His purpose was to seek money and to impose a tax on salt, which he had rightly estimated to be unpopular. Charles V and Charles VI levied taxes without the consent of the Estates, though it was the latter that gave their consent to the permanency of the taille and to the expenses necessary for the creation and the maintenance of a standing army, at their assembly at Orleans in 1439.

6. Fortescue's explanation is social: a conflict of interests. A Marxian interpreter, on the other hand, would see in it an instance of class-struggle. The official argument in favour of the nobles' exemption from the new taxes was the military service which they were expected to discharge in person.

7. A similar description had been included in DE LAUDIBUS, Ch. 35, 11, loc. cit., pp.82-85.

8. Whenever speaking of French prices and other rates, Fortescue renders them in "scutes" which have been translated into crowns here, for more convenience. Their value was 3s. 4d. apiece.

9. Although a relatively small part of the standing army, the franc-archers had been recruited from among the peasants, one from each parish. Their ranks were disbanded only after 1479. See Commynes, 5:19.

10. The contrast between the resources of the country and the poverty of the peasants in France is drawn by Fortescue to favour England by comparison and implicitly present the latter as the embodyment of a superior governing system aiming at universal welfare. He goes

so far as to imply that canvas was inferior to wool which was what the English wore. Actually, it was a matter both of climate and of the difference in staples between the two countries. While hemp was widely cultivated in France, in England there was a glut of lower grade wool during Fortescue's time, which lowered its price to an extent that made home consumption not only attractive but the only way out, as farmers kept buying sheep as a token of status. See also Lander (1977:35-36).

11.   ...jus regale.

12.   Isolation increases vulnerability and to compensate for it, increased self-reliance is needed. This is Fortescue's argument on which he rests the demand to meet the crown's extraordinary expenses, but also to institutionalize general conscription and to create a national reserve army, alongside a royal navy, the purpose of which was to defend the realm. Whereas traditionally, the obligation of those below the rank of knight had been to preserve the peace of their respective counties, Fortescue is shifting the ultimate purpose from the county to the realm as a whole. See also Powicke (1962: 216-223).

13.   Like the reference to Brutus, these too are ahistorical, being taken over from Geoffrey of Monmouth, 6: 1-5, or some other compilation inspired by it.

14.   According to tradition as recorded by Geoffrey of Monmouth, 8:20, Arthur was the son of the youngest of the three sons of Constantine, Uther Pendragon.

15.   The relative prosperity was largely due to a fact that Fortescue was not in a position to appreciate, namely, the low density of the population, which in turn raised the price of labour and the general living standard. That advantage would be lost in the following century. See Lander (1977:33-35).

16.   ...jus politicum et regale. This could be either a piece of propagandistic wishful thinking, or tongue-in-cheek irony, given the fact that only a short time

before, the English had lost all their French possessions, save Calais, and also that Henry VI had been unable to muster enough military forces, which would have
discouraged his barons from fighting each other and the
king and so would have kept the king's peace in rebel-
lious counties.

17.   ...ut(sic) ex fructibus eorum cognoscetis eos,
Matt. 7:16. This is another instance of the use which
Fortescue makes of a canonical authority to validate his
contrasting juxtaposition.

Chapter 4

1. This is the first time in the treatise, that Fortescue
speaks of kingship as office, albeit the king's office.
The concept is not new. Aquinas talks in similar terms
in DE REGIMINE, 1:15, for instance. The concept made its
way from Roman law into canon law with its papal doctrines about office and imperium. From there, it was
taken over by the new public or civil law to which
Fortescue was making his own contribution. In the present writing, he consistently treats kingship as office,
and the king as holder of that office and its executive.
In this way, he adopts an institutional approach of
the matter, from which personal idiosyncrasies of rulers
and even desirable personality traits in an ideal candidate are left out altogether, being replaced by con-
spicuous display, as it will be seen farther on. Fortescue's ideal monarch is the modern equivalent of the
chief executive officer, if one may say so.

2.   The two main functions which Fortescue associates
with the king's office, namely the defence of the realm
against external aggressors, and the protection of its
citizens through the enforcement of the law are mentioned in 1 Sam. 8:20. The Clermont edition reads somewhat
differently as regards the second function: "that he de-
fends his people against wrong-doers inward." Likewise,
it omits the biblical reference (Works, vol.I, p.453). On
the other hand, it is worth noting that the coronation
oath for Edward II (1308), and which in essence was used
until 1689, does not mention the defence of the realm, but

50

demands of the king to preserve the laws, customs and liberties for the clergy and the people, and peace and accord in God for the same and to fulfill his judiciary obligations: "with equal and right justice and discretion in mercy and truth," and finally to support and enforce the parliamentary legislation given during his reign. Fortescue eliminates any reference to Church and clergy, and changes the "accord in God" simply into administrative order, thus further secularizing the crown office. See also Brown (1989:12-13).

3. The Clermont edition condenses all this to: "which the French king does not". (Works, vol. I, p.453).

4. By resorting here to contrast to make his point, Fortescue renders himself guilty of contradiction by assimilating the administration of justice with fiscal policy.

5. This is one of the several instances in the treatise where Fortescue's power of argumentation fails him, and where to make up for it, he reverts to Christian moral injunctions.

6. ... per jus regale.

7. It refers to DE REGIMINE, 1:1. While earlier, in Chapter 2, tyranny is defined in terms of violence and arbitrary will, here the stress is shifted to personal profit and its pursuit, in ignorance and to the detriment of universal welfare, the good of all. In this way, it is the pursuit of public good that comes to distinguish a king from a tyrant in the eyes of Fortescue.

8. ...dominio regali. Herod the Great (d. 4 B.C.) had been declared king of Judea by the Roman Senate before he was able to take possession of his kingdom. Although a large part of his reign was taken by his successful attempts to remove his enemies and discourage rebellion, he was throughout accountable to the Roman imperial authorities for his acts and policies.

9. See Matt. 2:2-18.

10. ...quod principi placuit, legis habet vigorem. See

note 15 to Ch. 2, above. The principle applies only partially in the case of Herod, given the fact that he was a subject of the Romans who nominated him to the office within the boundaries of the Empire.

11.   Ahab, a historical figure, was the seventh king of Israel, successor of Omri, and who may be safely placed in the 9th century B.C., although the scholars disagree about the exact dates. To measure his deeds by the truncated principle taken from the Roman law does not pose any problem for the like of Fortescue who place their legal evidence sub specie aeternitatis, as God-given law. 1 Kings, 21:2-3.

12.   ...predic eis jus regis. See 1 Sam. 8:9-10.

13.   ...predic eis potestatem regis.

14.   In DE NATURA, 1:26, Fortescue acknowledges four categories of law: the law of God; the law of nature or of reason; positive law or man's law, and lastly, custom. The law of God is "whatever divine Providence is"(1:42), and in concrete terms, it is canon law. "The law of God rules the law of nature for ever" (1:39). One of his definitions of the law of nature in DE NATURA reads: "the law of nature is the truth of justice which is capable of being revealed by right reason"(1:26). As reason is divine, it may be said that canon law inspires and informs the law of nature, articulated to deal with novel situations for which no precedent could be found. The purpose of both is to dispose man to virtue, and so avoid mischief. On the other hand, the law of nature is the source of, and serves as authority for positive law and custom, which supplement it. Fortescue's recourse to canon law, to which he adds indiscriminately papal doctrines and principles from Roman law, however imperfect, has a precise technical purpose, namely to legitimize, that is to say, to lend his arguments and prescriptions the weight of the law of nature in the making, for the polity that he is witnessing as an insider. In a way, Fortescue also emulates the proceedings of the assembly of all the justices of England for matters of law, the function of which was to advise on points of law by argument. The assembly considered legal issues

concerning all kinds of law. The opinion of the majority was accepted unquestionably as the most authoritative pronouncement on such difficult legal questions. See also Chrimes (1972:159-160).

15.   Here his legalistic standpoint got the better of his political acumen as it makes him project a requisite of personal ethics upon the holder of a political office in pursuit of universal welfare. To adopt that Socratic recommendation and carry it out in action is a very difficult thing to ask of anybody. To ask it from the king as chief executive officer is beyond doubt to lead him to his demise. Henry VI might have tried just that, to the detriment of his authority as king, and at the expense of social order in his kingdom. To fail to distinguish between personal morality and political ethics while tackling issues that concern more than two people is guarantee for ill success. On the other hand, Fortescue's prescription may also to a degree be inter-preted as a recommendation to the king to acquire a bet-ter understanding of the situation of his subjects, mutually beneficial to the extent it fosters trust on both sides.

16.   This argument has no historical basis and does not explain the defeats of the French in the earlier stages of the Hundred Years' War. Its aim is merely to warn the reader of the negative consequences of any fiscal policy gone amiss.

17. In 1449, the Treasurer told Parliament that the king's debts had risen to £372,000, while the worth of the yearly income was but £5,000. See Lander (1977:66), as well as Wolffe (1970:92), among others.

18.   By "estate" it is here meant not only the king's position in the hierarchical network and the inherent functions of the office, but also patrimony and income-yielding prerogatives. It is the closest approximation of the concept of the state, which Fortescue comes to, without using that very term.

Chapter 5

1. The shortage of cash seems to have pestered mostly the Lancastrian kings, reaching a point of no return in the reign of Henry VI owing to a plurality of factors, among which a considerable trade recession and the decline in customs revenue, wasteful distribution of royal patronage and property and the reluctance of Parliament to grant taxes.

2. The interest on loans was high, indeed, and there is no reason to question Fortescue's accuracy on this matter, when he estimates the rate to range between 20 and 25 per cent.

3. This is a free translation of the technical term "chevisaunce" used by Fortescue. It defines the systematic disguise of formal usury, which was immoral and so condemned by the Church. The compounded interest was added to the actual loans and the lenders were credited at the Exchequer with larger sums that included the interest without for that matter recording it openly.

4. Thus Fortescue considers usury one of the vehicles of social change, affecting not only hierarchy but also property relations. In other words the cash nexus enables "sons of beggars" to become gentry.

5. The Clermont edition reads instead: "and yet it is left to his own surety" (Works, vol. I, p. 454).

6. Fortescue does attach utmost importance to material resources as the main stay of royal power and authority. In this context he is keen on underlining the weight acquired by the cash nexus that has been squeezing out both the honorial and the patronage systems from public administration in favour of contracting.

7. Something that Fortescue might have done himself as chief justice of the King's bench, though not on such a scale as Cardinal Beaufort who is estimated to have lent the crown in excess of £212,000 between 1404 and 1446. The process had two aspects to it: one was to extend credit to the crown by providing services for deferred payment, and the other, to make actual gifts, or aids, in excess of benevolences and other fees and taxes that

represented royal prerogatives, and in the form of payments made into the royal chamber or as advances to the Exchequer. In certain circumstances, the creditors could recoup part of their expenses through gifts that they were likely to receive, other advantages, by demanding a high rate of interest on the advances, or by surrendering their offices for a fee.

8. In principle, assignments were anticipatory drafts on revenue, and used to take different forms. One of them was a writ issued to a royal official expected to have money in hand, ordering him to satisfy a king's creditor from the reserves at his disposal. The writ was accompanied by a tally for the amount involved. The official was expected to present the tally for the money he had already paid on order from the king, when he went to Westminster to the Exchequer to account for his collections and disbursements. Eventually, the tallies could be traded, though at heavy discount. At times, there were no tallies, but the receiver had to surrender the writ to the official when paid, so that the latter could have some proof at hand to account to the Exchequer for the particular payment. Officials of the household departments would also issue bills or "debentures of the wardrobe" in exchange for cash they had received on request. Assignments could also be issued as letters under the great seal, that were duly recorded and enrolled. The system had been in force since the 12th century or even earlier. The frequency of assignments is an index of the strain on royal revenue, due either to abnormally large expenditure, or to a drastic reduction in revenue itself. As such assignments were regarded with disfavour because their bearers could never be sure of payment on presentation, particularly during periods of dearth and bad book-keeping: "Other payment get they none but a white stick". See Steel (1954:xxix-xxxiv).

9. The mark was a unit of value equal to 13s 4d, whereas there were 20s in the £.

10. That is to say, of cash in hand, as distinct from cash-yielding property, which through reckless alienation, worsened the former.

11.   ...impossible est indigentem operari bona. Fortescue's Latin source could not be identified, while his
command of Greek is a moot question. The quotation,
though, is close enough to the text of Aristotle's
NICOMACHEAN ETHICS, 1:8:15 (1099b). It is used in support of his pet opinion that poverty is socially and
politically disrputive, through the corruption which it
breeds. It is on this argument that Fortescue rests his
plea in favour of general welfare.

Chapter 6

1. See note 18 to Ch. 4, above. Here too, "estate" has
the meaning of the whole political and administrative
structure headed by the king as chief executive officer,
much in the way Machiavelli would talk about "stato," a
couple of decades later.

2. Here again Fortescue resorts to a canonical authority
and this time is St. Bernard of Clairvaux (1090-1153).
The text to which he refers, though, is of doubtful at-
tribution. It is possible that he first came to know of
it from a paraphrase in Scottish verse, in circulation
in written form during his lifetime, as BERNARDUS DE
CURA REGIMINE REI FAMILIARIS. It is an extensive epistle
on domestic economy, which is nowadays attributed to
Bernard Silvester (d. before 1160). The Latin text, reproduced by Lumby (1965:VI) from a 1640 Paris edition
reads as follows: "Audi ergo et attende quod si in domo
tua sumtus et redditus sunt aequales, casus inopinatus
poterit destruere statum ejus".

3. By ordinary charges Fortescue means regular, customary expenses, essential to the office of kingship and
which because of their steady recurrence could be fore-
cast. By extraordinary charges, on the other hand, it
should be understood irregular, symptomatic, unforesee-
able expenses, likely to be incurred by the crown at
any time.

4. Both kinds, however, are necessary, not only because
they define kingship materially as an institution, but
also because they are instrumental in keeping the nation

56

together. Fortescue assumes the delicate task of regulating royal expenditures, and at the same time, of convincing the tax-payers of the necessity to subscribe to the efficient implementation of the crown's official functions.

5. Fortescue often makes no distinction between livelihood, as property, overall wealth or capital, on the one hand, and on the other, income deriving from real and movable property, as well as from prerogatives and other taxes or subsidies. For the sake of clarity, more precise terms have been substituted for the too vague "livelihood".

6. That is by not having to pay interest on loans. Fortescue's wish that the crown should put an end to borrowing never came true, although both Edward IV and Henry VII were keen on following his advice.

7. In other words, good administration and self-sufficiency do not restrict sovereignty; on the contrary, they render the king less dependent on parliament on matters of solvency and related policies. On the other hand, sovereignty need not be equated with the patronage system. Rather, it is grounded on power which, in turn, presupposes material wealth, all the more important in the conditions of a political system within which remunerated, professional service is the functioning principle of its administration.

8. Fortescue's argumentation is here quite contorted. Actually, what he wants to say is simply that power increases with the reduction of one's imperfections.

9. As Chrimes (1937:41-53) has already shown, Fortescue uses the term "prerogative" in three ways: one, the king's prerogative, to mean sovereignty; a second, a prerogative of the king, meaning one of the king's privileges, and the third, the king's prerogatives, to mean the totality of the king's privileges. Here, he begins by referring to the first meaning, because it is by his sovereignty that the king is above all his subjects, only to switch to the second meaning in the next sentence, of prerogative as royal privilege.

10. This idea is resumed and extrapolated in Chapter 10.

11. The royal household (domus regia) was the social and economic organization of the royal court, concerned with the maintenace of the king's estate (i.e., status); it had its purchasing and spending departments, along- the wardrobe and the chamber, taking care not only of the king's person but also of his retainers, guests and visitors.

12. Fortescue favours a down-sized and more efficient royal household, the staff of which is to be fully dissociated from the advisory body connected with the king's policy-making office.

13. Purveyance was one of the main objects of discontent against the royal household, because of the abuse committed by the staffers for their own interests. It featured among the grievances aired during Cade's rebellion of 1450. Whence Fortescue's plea for its reform: acquisitions should be made exclusively to meet the needs of the king, and be paid promptly in cash, at market prices.

14. It was the Exchequer which received the accounts of the royal household. See Steel (1954:xxx).

15. The Clermont edition adds: "his guard and other servants" (Works, vol. I, p. 456).

16. That is, for the defence of the borders: the East March with the command of Berwick, and the West March with that of Carlisle, as well as a Middle March along the Scottish border, between the Cheviott Mountains, on the east, and Kirsop, on the west. The task was in the hands of wardens who, in time of war, would receive the double of the payments that were made to them in time of peace.

17. Fortescue seems to have been in favour of a reduction in the payments made to, and the special treatment which the wardens might have enjoyed, as he was suspecting them of profiteering and something akin to extortions. Royal control was relatively weak in the border area, in Fortescue's time, and he, a civilian of the new

gentry, had every reason to show dislike for the warring nobility that commanded those areas and showed little respect for royal justices.

18. Actually, the maintenance of Calais was only intermittently a burden on the country. At times, as Steel (1954:170) shows, cash was paid in the Exchequer on behalf of the city, in addition to revenue. It also happened that money was borrowed on behalf of Calais by, among other ways, sending commissioners into the counties to collect it. On the other hand, the garrison that was kept there was indeed costly, and a drain on the crown finances. Nonetheless, as England was at the time still looking towards the Continent and her people regarded the Channel as an English sea, there was no publicly expressed urge to surrender Calais to the French.

19.   The customary expenses covered repairs and maintenance of fortifications and the repair of royal buildings and amenities on crown property. It seems that each royal manor had a surveyor and/or a comptroller of the works, and sometimes even a clerk of works, attached to to it, in addition to the Clerk of the King's Works that received his livery with the Chancellor, the Treasurer and the other high officers of the crown. Indeed, forecasts of future expenses were difficult to make, unless one had accurate and comprehesive information not only about the state of repairs of the various structures, but also of the respective prices of labour and materials in each particular region, which was hardly the case in Fortescue's time. Like those other officials mentioned by him, the clerks and the surveyors of works had often to advance money for the construction work demanded of them, with little hope of ever being repaid. See Colvin (1963:1:189-201 and 2:1023-1024). New building projects, as they were not customary, are relegated by Fortescue to the category of extraordinary expenses, alongside defence and diplomacy.

20. Tonnage was a duty levied upon wine imported in tuns or casks at a certain rate for every tun. Poundage, on the other hand, was a duty levied on all exports and

imports, except bullion and the commodities subject to tonnage, usually at the rate of 12 pence in the £. Together, the two duties had first been levied in the 14th century, and as a rule, were granted by Parliament for the safeguarding of the sea. It seems, however, that whenever granted the subsidy, both Henry V and Henry VI, and later Edward IV, would use it loosely. By insisting on its customary purpose, Fortescue only repeats one of the demands which were submitted to Edward IV by his opponents in 1469.

21. Fortescue takes this opportunity to vent his displeasure with the magnates, who during the minority of Henry VI, sold away his father's great ships as an expedient. Eventually that decision came to be regarded as the demise of England's power at sea. The expansion of the royal navy was an expense that both Henry VI and Edward IV could ill afford. They tended to supplement their relatively small fleet by requisitioning merchantmen that were usually built in such a way as to be fit not only to carry cargo, but also to defend themselves against pirates. Such a royal habit had disruptive consequences for trade, with loss to all those involved.

22. Carracks were large, long-distance cargo vessels, with high decks, three or four masts and poops at each end, equipped to serve as ships of war, and widely used in Fortescue's time by the Portuguese.

Chapter 7

1. Although fully aware of the general reluctance to pay taxes on personal property and subsidize the country's administration, Fortescue has too much sense not to realize that it is quite impractical to exempt all the subjects all the time from materially contributing to their collective defence and their safety at home. He goes even farther to foster the idea that sharing in the national burden might be the bond that would keep the polity together. It is implicit in his notion of political dominion. It is the misuse of revenue from aids and taxes by the crown and the royal household that Fortescue objects to, because it undermines the trust in royal

authority and breeds indifference to the country's plights.

2. The reference is to the General Councils of the Roman Church, which in the first half of the 15th century, tried without success to reform it, particularly with regard to the locus of the supreme jurisdictional authority within the church. The Councils took place at Pisa (1409), Constance (1414-1418), Pavia-Siena (1423-1424), and Basel-Ferrara-Florence (1431-1449). They were attended by representatives of the clergy and also by royal envoys. Thus, Henry IV sent ambassadors to the Council of Pisa, and Henry V, to the Council of Constance, though his son, Henry VI, seems to have encountered difficulties when he tried to represent himself as King of France, at the Basel Council. At times, some attending cleric was asked to represent the king's interests also, or the royal envoys would be advised to secure the services of a permanent advocate in the Council, on behalf of the king, to apply himself to the king's matters there. The Conciliar theories might have influenced Fortescue's views on political dominion, though he was sensible enough not to reduce the king to a mere executive of the decisions taken by parliament.

3. The Clermont edition reads: "great councils", instead (Works, vol. I, p. 457). What Fortescue must be referring to here are the city-states of Italy, such as Venice, Genoa, Florence, and the like.

4. Diplomacy and the foreign service were not yet fully developed, permanent institutions, as they are included among the irregular expenses on Fortescue's list.

5. This is a reference to the inalienability of the royal patrimony, a principle upon which Fortescue insists time and again. See, for instance, Chapter 19.

6. That is to say, in cash, out of surplus liquidity, deposited in the treasury of the chamber. In the last years of Henry VI's reign, the collection of revenue as one of the functions of the chamber was revived at the expense of the Exchequer of Receipt, with the appointment of the treasurer of the royal chamber as the deputy

of the Treasurer of the Exchequer, to fulfill the function of receiver-general of the king's revenues.

7. The term "wealth" has been here employed instead of Fortescue's "tresour", in order to avoid confusion. It does not mean "treasury", but simply "abundance of cash".

8. Here Fortescue tries to justify two things: on the one hand, such expenses that may be called expenses of representation, related to the display of a certain life-style as it was expected of the holder of the kingly office, and on the other, ostentation in the monarch, materialized in the purchase of luxury goods, as well as jewelry and plate, not only as investment but also as securities and prizes. The luxury which Fortescue concedes to his monarch contrasts greatly with the legendary shabbiness displayed by Louis XI of France, for instance. Fortescue wants to enhance the king's image both as a component of royal authority, and to define the relationship between the crown and the new gentry serving it and seeking its support, at the expense of the magnates. Edward IV, who was fond of display and ostentation, apparently heeded his advice.

9. The Clermont edition reads "a private person", instead (Works, vol. I, p. 458).

10. That is, belts.

11. Fortescue must be speaking from personal experience, as one of the judges sent to investigate riots, treasons and assaults from Cornwall to Lincolnshire, and from Wales to Kent. Worthy of notice here is Fortescue's advocacy in favour of the organization of punitive armed forces, available to and under the command of the king, apart from the usual commissions of oyer et terminer.

12. Apparently, the obligation was limited to one's county and for a definite length of time. In rest, military service was payable. The basis for a mercenary army had already been in place, despite Fortescue's criticism of the principle when speaking of the kings of France. The services of a standing army of paid

professionals could not be efficiently replaced by those
of a retroactive national levy of reservists, a fact
which Fortescue seems reluctant to admit, out of his
displeasure as a man of law, and also perhaps, remember-
ing the composition of the forces used by Henry V in his
French campaigns. See also Powicke (1962:244-250).

13.   Several things are implied here: one is the inability of Parliament to take quick decisions; another is
a hint to the reluctance of the propertied classes to
comply with parliamentary decisions, in particular with
regard to subsidies and impositions; still another is
the need of considerable cash reserves that would ap-
proximate a modern, permanent, state budget, under the
king's control. Relatedly, the king's advance payments
for military campaigns could have worked to a degree as
an inducement upon the subjects to make their own financial contribution to the military expenses, being guaranteed that their money would be spent to no other
purpose. Lastly, Fortescue conveys the precariousness
of the king's position vis-à-vis his subjects, and
the vulnerability of the realm as a whole in case of
foreign intervention.

Chapter 8

1.   See also note 4 to Chapter 6,above. The reference is
to the cash surplus that is returned to the king after
the expenses have been earmarked.

2.   Here Fortescue merely reiterates a general opinion
held by his class, and namely, that the crown as office
had been well provided for institutionally, through
legislation, at the time of the foundation of the kingdom. Whence to regain those forfeited parameters should
be one of the king's main concerns, and in which, as it
will be shown further on, the support of parliament and
the advice of experts was to be secured.

3.   ...rex datur propter regnum, et non regnum propter
regem. See DE REGIMINE, 3:11, where the difference between royal dominion and political dominion is discussed.
The Latin paraphrase could be Fortescue's, already

reproduced both in DE NATURA 1:25 and in DE LAUDIBUS, ch. 30, 11:22-24, loc. cit., pp. 88-89.

4. See Chapter 4, above, and notes 1 and 2 to it, about the functions which Fortescue associates with the royal office.

5. ...servus servorum dei. It is Bede (673-735) in his ECCLESIASTICAL HISTORY, 1:23-24, who reproduces letters of Pope Gregory the Great with this superscription. Bede's work was a canonical authority of wide circulation, with which Fortescue must have been familiar, although he uses the quotation to make a different point. Whereas Gregory had been trying to reassure both the local bishops and the princes in England of his good intentions, and attenuate their fears of Rome's ambitions to win supremacy over them, Fortescue presents it as a definition that may be applied to the office of the secular head of the realm. The parallel between the office of the pope and the office of the king is drawn in order to legitimize the obligation of each member of the community to contribute to its preservation and perpetuation, among other things, by assuring the good-functioning of the kingly office. What follows is a whole battery of quotations from the New Testament brought in, as authority, to enforce his argument.

6. ...nemo debet propriis expensis militare. It is a paraphrase of 1 Cor. 9:7. The Vulgate text reads: "Quis militat suis stipendiis umquam?"

7. ...dignus est operarius cibo suo. Slight paraphrase of Matt. 10:10.

8. communicet (autem) ist qui catechizatur verbo, ei qui se catechizat, in omnibus bonis. The Apostle in question is St. Paul and the quotation is from Gal. 6:6. The Clermont edition omits this sentence altogether. (Works, vol.I, p. 459)

Chapter 9

1. This is but a repetition of the beginning of the previous chapter.

2. Actually, Fortescue speaks of two lords and so does the Clermont edition (Works, vol.I, p.459). Plummer (1885:128), though, replaces the two by one, which makes the comparison hard to grasp. Besides, it is more than likely that Fortescue was anxious to remain discreet about the identity of the magnates: had he chosen Plummer's alternative, that lord could have easily been identified with Richard, Duke of York (1411-1460), known as the richest noble of the realm, his former declared enemy, and father to the king to whom eventually he dedicated the treatise.

3. See Chapter 5, p. 9, above, where Fortescue shows that an impecunious king is likely to be forsaken by his subjects who would follow someone able to pay their expenses.

4. This refers to the actual income, and not the ideal which would not only cover the ordinary expenses but also yield a surplus. In the treatise, Fortescue takes a first step to render the ideal practical by his attempt to convince both the king and his free subjects, irrespective of rank, of the wisdom and feasibility of his recommendations. See also Chapter 4, above.

5. ...omnia amamus sed principari maius. Whether in this case, Fortescue means Aristotle when he mentions "the philosopher", or simply uses a rhetorical device to introduce a household saying is anybody's guess. It may also be a corruption of meaning, through a faulty Latin translation, of the principle reproduced by Aristotle in his POLITICS, 7:3:4 (1325a), namely, "The best is most desirable: and 'to do well' is the best." See also Plummer (1885:225).

6. As earlier in Chapter 5, Fortescue underlines the importance of the cash nexus in the relation between prince and his subjects. In that light, what Fortescue identifies as freedom and "a better law" in Chapter 3 is outright pragmatism that becomes apparent in any period of transition.

7. Fortescue's historical references, unless concerned with immediate history, are far from accurate, made as

they are to serve legitimizig purposes. Evidence which could pass muster among his contemporaries was all that he needed to enforce his arguments: it was the authority of the source and not its authenticity that concerned him.

8. The last Merovingian king, Childeric III (d.754 A.D.) had been deposed by Pippin the Short in 751 and banished to the monastery of Sithiu.

9. Clovis I (465-511 A.D.), king of the Franks, was converted to Christianism round 496, most likely under the influence of his wife Clotilde, herself a Christian.

10. Charles Martel (688?-741 A.D.) became majordomo of the palace under the last Merovingians, and through a coup, eventually the effective ruler of the realm, defending it against the perils of disintegration at the expense of its neighbours. The victory scored at Poitiers in 732/3 against the Arab invasion of Abd-el-Rahman confirmed his authority and enabled him to found his own dynasty by securing the succession to the throne of his sons Pippin and Carloman.

11. The reference must be to Charles, Duke of Lower Lorraine (953?-992?), uncle of the deceased king Louis V, the last of the reigning Carolingians. As such, he was claiming his hereditary right to the throne, but was captured and imprisoned by the newly annointed king, Hugo Capet.

12. Hugo I Capet (941?-996) was the first king of the Capetian dynasty brought to the French throne by the machinations of the archbishop of Reims, Adalberon, at the death of Louis V.

13. Hugo the Great (897?-956), Count of Paris and Duke of the Franks, was father to Hugo I Capet.

14. The reference is to Charles the Bold (1433-1467), Duke of Burgundy, who as Count of Charolais, had laid siege to the city of Paris during the War of the Public Weal in 1465, thus embarassing king Louis XI of France, in his own house.

15. It is quite probable that Fortescue has in mind the risings of Richard, Duke of York, and his confederates against Henry VI, that led to the enthronement of Edward IV in 1461, and the subsequent rebellion against the latter, which brought about the brief readeption of Henry VI in 1470, to say nothing of his Scottish and Continental experiences.

16. Respectively, Simon of Montfort (1208?-1265) and Gilbert de Clare (1243-1295), who as leaders of the baronial party, defeated Henry III at the battle of Lewes in May 1264, when the latter and his son Edward surrendered to Gloucester.

17. That is to say, James II, king of Scotland (1430-1460), and James, Earl of Douglas (1426-1488), younger brother of William Douglas. The latter had apparently been stabbed by the king himself in February 1452, in retribution for his disruptive and anarchical conduct as the richest magnate of the realm. On inheriting the earldom, James Douglas showed himself as anarchical in his behaviour. Eventually, in the aftermath of a failed rebellion against the king, in 1454, Douglas took refuge in England where he became a pensioner of the English kings. Thirty years later, while crossing the border into Scotland, on a dispatch on behalf of Edward IV, he was caught and sentenced to perpetual banishment to the Abbey of Lindores where he died four years later.

18. They were four, because in the Vulgate, the two books of Samuel were coded as 1 and 2 Kings. The Clermont edition goes on to conclude this sentence as follows: "wherefore it needs not to write more herein" (Works, vol.I, p. 460).

19. It is under this condition, as intrinsic manifestationt of universal welfare, free of political ambitions, that Fortescue tolerates vast accummulations of wealth outside the royal patrimony.

20. The Clermont edition reads: "a great duke", instead. The reference is to John of Gaunt (1340-1399), fourth son of Edward III, who in virtue of his second marriage to Constance, elder daughter of the deceased king of Castile,

Pedro the Cruel, claimed Castile, on the basis of female succession. At the beginning, he did so only nominally, but later, in 1386, he set up an expedition to occupy Castile, which eventually ended with his withdrawal into Bayonne. In the long run, a settlement was reached with the king of Castile who married one of John of Gaunt's daughters, defrayed the costs of Gaunt's expedition and granted him and the duchess an annuity for life. In return, John of Gaunt gave up his claim to the title of king of Castile.

21.   The chapter ends as it began: with an emphasis on the insecurity that feeds on that kind of authority which is undermined by inadequate material means. In Fortescue's case, repetition is a didactical device, to impress his point on his reader's mind.

Chapter 10

1.   A rather simple working hypothesis lies behind this somewhat strained juxtaposition: a centralized state is likely to yield more income to its government than one ridden by factional strife and divided among magnates that enjoy local autonomy.

2.   In mid 13th century, there were six spiritual and six temporal peers, headed by the Archbishop of Reims, who as a court, seem to have fulfilled important judiciary functions, though later, were reduced to merely ceremonial functions on such occasions as the coronation of the kings of France. The twelve peers were: the dukes of Normandy, Burgundy and Guyenne, the counts of Flanders, Champagne and Toulouse, and the bishops of Langres, Laon, Chalons-sur-Marne, Bauvais and Noyon, who were vassals to the king, in virtue of their titles. Loss of autonomy and the English occupation in the 14th century put an end to the institution.

3.   The Clermont edition adds: "and still is". (Works, vol. I, p. 461)

4.   In the Clermont edition the price is limited to two shillings. (Works, vol.I, p. 461)

5.   Much of the salt used in England was imported from the bay of Bourgneuf, south of the Loire estuary, while wine came mostly from Gascony. The loss of the French territories put an end to cheap sources of the two staples, and made salt a permanent issue in the negotiations and the agreements between the two countries.

6.   The gabelle had already been discussed in DE LAUDIBUS, ch. 35, 11:15-21, loc. cit., pp. 82-83.

7. The reference here is to sales and consumption taxes which were unknown in England at the time.

8.   Ultimately, Fortescue is not as reluctant to the introduction of such taxes as it seems at first sight. He even goes so far as to suggest that opposition to new and permanent taxes might be undermined by their universal application to all social ranks of traders and consumers, unlike in France where the nobility was exempt of taxes.

9.   ...a me factum est istud. This is a free Latin paraphrase, possibly Fortescue's, of 1 Kings, 12:24. King Solomon reigned between 962? and 931 B.C., spending heavily, particularly on his court and standing army. His expenses were financed in part through taxes which affected the agricultural north of his realm most severly. Rehoboam, the first king of Judah, after the division, was a son of Solomon, who succeeded his father at the age of forty-one. He reigned for seventeen years, until his death, round 912 B.C.. Rehoboam failed to quell Israel's riot against his decision to continue Solomon's policy of heavy taxation and reduce Israel by force as a consequence.

10.   Canon law rendered rebellion against overtaxation legitimate, and so placed any Christian monarch in a difficult position.

11.   This is a prescription for an efficient, rational administration of the crown patrimony and also, though indirect, for the neutralization of the practice of uses, widespread in Fortescue's time, and by which tenants were alienating their holdings at will, with losses of

prerogatives for the kings. See Bean (1968:216-234).

12.   In virtue of his right to marriages, the king enjoyed part of the use of the potential dowry of the
brides-to-be and perceived a fee from the future bride-
grooms to allow them to marry his wards. The Earl of
Warwick (1428-1471), one of the two greatest magnates of
the time, did indeed augment his estate through the
dowry of his wife, whereas the Duke of York profited
hugely by his maternal inheritance. What Fortescue advocates here is the reactivation of crown privileges
with a view to their efficient economic exploitation in
favour of the kingly office, and for the general welfare
of the nation. What he wants is to build up new custom
through the reinterpretation of precedent, with the
advice of legal experts and the support of the commons
in parliament.

13.   That is to say, people in the king's employ, retainers. The king could not be a tenant in virtue of his
office, as he was meant to serve his realm as a whole.
On the other hand, before Henry VI's reign, the Lancastrians, from John of Gaunt to Henry V, had consistently the largest number of retainers in the country under
their control. It has been estimated that the annuities
granted by Henry IV in 1401 to those in his service,
for instance, amounted to £24,000 a year. See Pugh
(1972:107-108).

14.   This implies not only a systematic resumption of
land and real estate grants and the confiscation of the
property of those found guilty of treason against the
crown, but also a kind of sumptuary legislation regarding real estate, that would set the limits on individual
property according to a scale to be devised, and with
the crown enjoying the largest part.

15.   It was one of the means by which the crown attempt-
ed to protect its prerogatives against the process of
extensive alienation through uses of the property held
from the king by his tenants with the consequent loss of
such rights of his as wardship, marriage, seisin, escheat, patronage, etc. Moreover, it was also used as a

source of ready money, and a means to control the circulation of property. Fines could be imposed retroactively for failure to apply for the permission. Fortescue's recommendation is for the crown to appropriate the alienable holdings of its tenants.

16.   The Clermont edition reads instead: "may not for his honour sell his land." (Works, vol.I, p. 462) As a matter of fact, the contrary is true: kings could indeed buy and sell property at pleasure and not limit themselves to exchanges. This is a moot point in Fortescue's doctrine of inalienable crown patrimony, and the only instance in the whole treatise where he tries to impose a restriction on a royal prerogative. His awareness of the inalienability of royal domains in France might have fortified him in the conviction of the practical value of the restriction as a preventive measure against royal prodigality.

17.   The castle and lordship of Chirk in Northern Wales had been bought by Henry V from his grand-mother, Joan de Bohum and incorporated in the earldom of Chester. The latter was then raised to the rank of a principality and inalienably appropriated to the eldest son of the king. Eventually, Henry VI sold them alongside other estates to Cardinal Beaufort, his great-uncle, in 1438/9. At the latter's death, they were inherited by his nephew Edmund, Earl of Somerset (d.1455). They reverted to the crown, following the Beauforts' attainder in 1464. Edward IV then granted them to Sir William Stanley and his male heirs, without being able to foresee that it would be through Stanley that the House of York would come to an end. Nor could Fortescue foresee it.

Chapter 11

1.   Genesis, 47:14-26.

2.   In this context Babylon is synonimous with Cairo. Plummer (1885:276) identifies the Sultan as Qa'it Bay (d.1496) of the Mameluke Circassian dynasty. Actually, he was the head of a centralized state, efficiently administered and who consequently was able to resist the

Turks throughout his reign. The biblical continuity assumed by Fortescue is doubtful. Indeed, the Islamic
traditions had allowed Muhammad the fifth part of the
booty taken by his followers, but whether the quota had
been set under the influence of the biblical tradition
or whether it was a pre-Islamic, Arabian custom taken
over by the warriors of Islam is impossible to ascertain
here.

3. Thus Fortescue reiterates his preference for uniform
and continuous taxation, as well as a permanent, national budget which should represent one fifth of the gross
national product, and turns once again to canon law for
authoritative confirmation of the validity of his pro-
position.

4. The way in which Fortescue figures out the institutionally established wealth of the English crown is
quite fantastic, though perhaps it did not seem so to
the canonists who used to look for practical answers to
their queries in the bible. Nonetheless, I find strange
the way he ignores an actual Anglo-Saxon legacy, taken
over by the Norman conquerors, namely the royal geld or
Danegeld. It had been a regular royal taxation applied
to all the lands in England, irrespective of the status
and the arrangements of their holders. See also Wolffe
(1971:23)

5. The reference is to that kind of estates of inheritance, in which the tenant had only a life interest in
his estate. On his death, it reverted to the heir, and
in the absence of a heir, to the representative of the
original donor. In consequence, lands held in fee tail
could be forfeited only for the life-time of the tenant
who committed the crime, whether it was treason or something else. Afterwards, they returned to his heirs. What
follows is a more or less systematic list of the legitimate and illegitimate forms of alienation of crown
property, with the substitution of payments in ready
money by others in immovable property as the most nox-
ious.

6. In other words, Fortescue advocates the overall replacement of the patronage and honour systems by a

contract system, which in turn, implies rational estate management and cash nexus. Rewards in perpetuity are to be put an end to and be replaced by grants of cash and leases for varying terms, but not exceeding the term of life. These payments, this is what they are after all, are not to be made without the advice of the council and the assent of parliament. In the long run it was king Henry VII who adopted measures approximating Fortescue's recommendations to a degree. Fortescue's aim is to put an end to alienation of crown patrimony and to abolish hereditary tenure. Resumption on a large scale, on the other hand, had already been discussed in parliament during Henry V's reign and even earlier. However, it was the Parliament of February 1449 that asked for a full resumption of royal grants, which became law as the Resumption Act of May 1450. It was enacted with some success both in the later years of Henry VI's reign and during Edward IV's. See Wolffe (1971: 140) and also Lander (1977:67). On the other hand, the practice of granting a money fee instead of land for services had been in use from the 11th century on. If originally it had served as a means of military recruitment, the contract system, which gradually developed out of it, does indeed justify Fortescue in his recommendation to generalize it. See also Bean (1989:123).

7.   Mostly tonnage and poundage or other trade taxes, because of a general reluctance to pay taxes on personal property.

Chapter 12

1.   England in the 15th century was a sanguinary land, and riots, rebellions, revolts, skirmishes and the like were quite frequent, though perhaps the most famous of all was Cade's in 1450, and eventually, the armed confrontations among the barons, known under the more recent, collective name of the War of the Roses.

2.   ...ad pauca respicientes de facili enunciat.

3.   The Clermont edition adds "mostly" as a qualifier. (Works, vol.I, p. 464)

4. The Hundred Years' War created the conditions for the organization of a national militia, through the recruitment and training of archers from among free men. The Parliament at Reading in March 1453 granted the crown a force of 20,000 archers for six months's service, for the defence of the realm. See Storey (1966:103).

5. A jack is a sleeveless leather tunic or jacket, quilted or plated with iron and worn by foot soldiers.

6. Free men between the ages of 16 and 60 were required to possess arms and practise the use of arms with their own equipment, according to a statute of 1285. See Lander (1977:161). Their assessment was made according to the size of their property. Thus, bows and arrows were listed among the weapons of those owning £10 of land and less.

7. Here Fortescue renders himself guilty of inconsistency. Compare this statement of his about poverty as cause of rebellion to what he has written in Chapter 9, pp. 17-18, where the initiative for rebellion is attributed to the rich.

8. The reference is to the Hussite wars of 1419-1436. In keeping with his overall approach to the matters discussed in the treatise, Fortescue links them to social causes, in this case - the deprivation of the commons by the nobility.

9. Thus Fortescue adds the guarantee of the welfare of the whole nation to the other main functions of the kingly office, namely, the judiciary and the military. Eventually, he turns it into the first objective of the king's governance. See also Chapter 4 above, and note 2 to it. The concept is not new, indeed. Plato in THE REPUBLIC (10:15), Aristotle, and later, Aquinas stressed its importance for law and politics. Plummer (1885:285-286) attributes to Fortescue a reinterpretation of the idea about the obligation of the king to rule in a way by which his subjects would be well provided to Aegidius Romanus. The notion was in wide circulation during Fortescue's time, and although it would be impossible to put the finger on Fortescue's source for it, it pervades

both DE LAUDIBUS and the present treatise. It not only informs the law of nature and is the objective of governance, but also serves as standard for measuring the relationship between king and subjects.

10.   See note 2 to Chapter 4 and note 9 to this chapter. To protect the citizens and their property is Fortescue's secularized rendition of the coronation oath. Under this new form, his objective has survived to become one of the functions of the modern state.

11.   A fifteenth and a tenth were temporary taxes levied on movable, personal property, in those proportions, in shires and boroughs, respectively, for the benefit of the crown.

12. These are taxes on revenue, like the fifteenth and the tenth and not sales taxes.

13.   This is a repetition of the opinion that pauperization on an extensive social scale is likely to breed political disorganization, expressed in Chapter 5, above.

14.   It is not the injustice of inequality, in the modern, conventional sense of the phrase, that Fortescue talks about here. Rather it is a plea in favour of an impartial and effective administration of justice, which in his opinion, could equitably resolve complaints against forcible or arbitrary transfers of property, and implement the related decisions.

Chapter 13

1.   In the light of the ultimate purpose of the treatise, this chapter is superfluous. It is more or less an expansion of Fortescue's argument in favour of general prosperity, guaranteed by an effective system of justice, from yet another vantage point, namely, psychological. From the psychological discussion that follows, the element worth retaining is the persistence of idiosyncrasies that contribute to the differentiation of communities among themselves, which Fortescue upholds. On the other hand, his analysis of criminality in England,

France and Scotland is interesting in itself, coming as it does from a judge of criminal cases, who was also blessed with a sense of humour.

2.   The Caux region is situated in Normandy, on the northern bank of the Seine.

3.   Indeed, Fortescue's fanciful, psychological interpretation of the rebellion of Caux lists the same motives which he later attributes to the thieves in Scotland! Essentially, in his opinion, it is fear which is the determining factor that turns people into conformists and law-abiders.

4.   Actually what Fortescue, very likely tongue in cheek, describes as courage in his fellow countrymen is but anarchical individualism, in modern terms.

5.   Thus, inadvertently, Fortescue has come to appreciate the low rate of crime with intent to rob, that prevailed in France during his exile there, despite his high-faluting, psychological explanation of it.

Chapter 14

1.   The Clermont edition reads "act of Parliament", instead. (Works, vol.I, p. 467) See note 6 to Chapter 11, above. The proposal is far less radical than it purports.

2.   For the structure and functions of the consultative council, as envisaged by Fortescue, see Chapter 15 and Appendix I.

3.   Two new recommendations are brought in at this point. One, that rewards to worthy subjects should be counted among the extraordinary expenses, and so be paid out of the national revenue, and not the king's patrimony. In this way, an incipient distinction is drawn between the king's household proper, on the one hand, and the crown's administrative officers or civil servants, on the other. The second recommendation is about the advisory role assigned to the king's council in the selection of candidates for rewards. Alongside the invocation of the authority of parliament, this recommendation has been

Interpreted as another limitation on the monarch's sovereignty. Given the importance which Fortescue attaches to the latter, one is inclined to differ, and see them, instead, as technical devices meant to prevent any occupant of the kingly office from dissipating its attributes and so bring it into a state past repair. Both parliament and council are turned into legitimating bodies in the distribution of rewards. What Fortescue would like to see, though, is the curbing of royal munificence, a traditional prerogative, and its replacement by a rational system of compensation based on merit, for the implementation of which parliament would be made partially responsible.

4. See Chapter 11, above.

5. It seems here that Fortescue has in mind the appointment of a special committee to deal with grants, compensations and payments, distinct from the advisory council. See also Appendix I.

6. Hence the need of bringing to light allegedly old royal prerogatives, and restating them in the changed circumstances.

7. That is to say, traffic of influence. Plummer (1885: 309) elegantly translates the term by "undue influence".

8. ...ubi multa consilia, ibi salus. It may be a paraphrase of the Vulgate text: Ubi non est gobernator, populus corruet: salus autem, ubi multa consilia (Prov.11: 14).

9. ... multa consilia.

10. The notion of a "continual council" gained circulation in the later part of the 14th century. See Chrimes (1952:244-245).

Chapter 15

1. The king's council included the great officers of the realm alongside the magnates, members of the royal family and the lords of the church and very few, if any, commoners. It enjoyed executive powers, and whenever the

77

monarch was unable to exercise his official functions for whatever reason, it acted as a deliberative body, too. On the other hand, the council envisaged by Fortescue would be a different body altogether: purely advisory, as it excludes the great officers, its members would be recruited for their ability and impartial professionalism, irrespective of status or income. This advisory council would serve the monarch exclusively and without intermediaries, its purpose being to consolidate the king's office and position vis-à-vis the magnates and the commons alike, by supplying expert knowledge and advice for the resolution of issues at stake and in the general administration of the realm.

2. This emphasis on the need of discretion and even of secrecy in politics shows what a sensible politician Fortescue was, given the overall precarious conditions, characterized by open acess at court, the absence of a country-wide police force and counterintelligence, and the widespread use of rumour as a news medium and propaganda ploy.

3. Corodies or corrodies were payments usually but not exclusively made in kind by religious houses to persons nominated by the representative of the original founder. On the other hand, "pensions of abbeys" were perquisites paid by abbeys out of benefices which they administered and which could be retained at the disposal of the crown.

4. Such criteria of recruitment as individual talent and expertise would among other things widen the range of legal counsel available to the king, to cover not only canon and Roman law, but also the law of nature, civil law and custom.

5. One may see in this the beginnings of a code of conduct for the civil service. Bean (1986:219) is of the opinion that in Edward IV's second reign a sense of "lawful service" to the king was developing among those in his employ, below the rank of magnate. The idea of sworn servants to the king in exclusivity rests with the early Lancastrians, Henry IV and Henry V, who emulated John of Gaunt and turned the oath of office into a

policy both to control retaining and to secure a reliable following of their own. See Bean (1986:210-211).

6.   Fortescue has mentioned the judges' oath and its contents already in DE LAUDIBUS, 51:21-34, loc. cit., pp. 126-127. Seemingly, it was institutionalized during the reign of Edward III, c.1347.On the other hand, the King's Bench and the Common Pleas were two of the three central courts of the realm. The former dealt with matters that affected the king's interests, and as such, was mainly a criminal court, whereas the latter was a civil court. The Common Pleas dealt with cases between subject and subject, or said differently, it used to hear pleas between subjects. It was called "Common Pleas" in keeping with the status of the litigants and was concerned with real actions, such as ownership and tenure, debt and contracts. The third central court, the oldest of them all, was that of the Exchequer, which in the 15th century, had been reduced to handling "revenue" cases. All three courts set at Westminster during Fortescue's time.

7.   The principle to remove a councillor by majority vote preceded Fortescue, though it gained wide circulation in his lifetime. The rolls of the Parliament for 1429, for instance, specifically provided that punishment and removal of any councillor or great officer was to proceed by the assent and advice of the majority of all those appointed to the council. See Chrimes (1936: 133-137).

8.   This seems to be another of the very few concessions which Fortescue makes to the magnates. Henry VII might have been inspired by Fortescue's recommendation when, in 1487, he set up his tribunal or judicial council, made up of two or three great officers assisted by a temporal and a spiritual lord, the latter usually a bishop, recruited from among the king's councillors. This tribunal was distinct from the king's council, and fulfilled both advisory and judiciary functions. See Chrimes (1972:154-156)

9.   ...capitalis consiliarius. Moreover, while the members of Fortescue's council of professionals are to

serve for life, its chair is to be held by rotation.

10. This is the only instance in the treatise, in which Fortescue openly and unreservedly recommends the adoption of a French institution.

11. ...consiliarii nati. What Fortescue goes on to say is that the king's closest relatives need to be paid only for their attendance at the council's sessions. Any piece of advice proffered by any one of them outside the council's sessions should be free, given the fact that their own interests were intertwined with the king's. It is Fortescue's conviction that if applied, such a principle would discourage the transfer of crown assets to the highest magnates.

12. Some of the notables serving on the king's council during Henry VI's reign had already volunteered to give their attendance during term free. On the other hand, the various crown officers derived a substantial income from the fees they received for various services rendered in virtue of their offices. Accordingly, in Fortescue's time, sheriffs were not a model of selfless probity, but rather the opposite, whence also the limitation in time of their tenure to one year. What they did not get in the form of salaries from the king was made good by what outsiders perceived as extortions, abuse of power, and in general, partiality. The qualifications in terms of real property and inheritance within the corresponding counties, which a candidate for the office had to meet, were less criteria of status and respectability, than a kind of bond, a guarantee, against any complaint brought before the king against any of the sheriffs.

13. Given their complete dependency on the king for their offices.

14. On the one hand, this council of experts is meant to concern itself with matters of public administration, and on the other, has to formulate questions of general policy, of which finance, trade and the treatment of aliens are of special interest, alongside internal order. Fortescue is particularly concerned with the preservation

and increase of liquidity inside the country, as well as of the reserves of precious metals, which as bullion, could easily be minted into coins, or which in the form of objects, could serve as standard security for loans, and implicitly, as movable capital investment.

15.   Fortescue speaks here of what nowadays is known as the balance of payments. He seems to have shared his contemporaries' conviction that a favourable balance could be secured for a long duration in time through artificial intervention which in turn would discourage imports and the home consumption of exportable luxury goods, manufactured in the realm. The whole idea betrays a marked self-centrism in matters of consumption, offer and demand, and ignorance of the forces at play in the international markets of the time. One may also read into the text the commons' dissatisfaction with their monarchs' penchant for extravagance, as well as that of their households, as it often implied the purchase of very expensive luxury goods from abroad. It was regarded as one of the causes of the crown's chronic shortage of cash, and a drain on its financial resources.

16.   For the extraordinary expenses of the king see Chapter 7, above.

17.   Here Fortescue states once more the general purpose of practical politics, as he understood it, namely, to maximize national prosperity and well-being.

18.   In this way Fortescue assigns parliament a legitimate function, while reserving a probouleutic function to the council of experts. Both are meant to consolidate the king's sovereignty. The king could not alter the law or make new laws on his own, save during states of exception. Nonetheless, he kept the initiative throughout: it was he who summoned the parliament at his pleasure; submitted draft bills, or ammendations to older bills, and selectively enacted the bills already passed. Moreover, he enjoyed the freedom of discarding any inconvenient points in the final formulation of the bills, a task usually incumbent on his judges, and which did not require any resubmission to parliament.

Although intent on increasing the commons' political responsibility, Fortescue was well aware, as former MP, of the scant political experience and acumen which the commons of his times, gathered in parliament, did have, and also of the lack of any system and sense of urgency in their debates.

19.   Thus the great officers of the realm are excluded from the council of experts, which is given the authority to seek their opinion or make them give evidence on particular issues. Only the chancellor is conceded the favour of taking the chair at the sessions to which he is invited. See Appendix I for Fortescue's rather wary attitude towards chancellors, based on his own experience as civil servant.

20.   The Clermont edition erroneously reads: "may be conceived by leisure", instead. (Works, vol.I, p. 470)

Chapter 16

1.   The Roman Senate and its government was previously referred to in DE NATURA, 1:23.

2.   Meaning Gaius Julius Caesar (100-44 B.C.), who had never been an emperor, after all.

3.   That is, Octavian Augustus (63 B.C.-14 A.D.), who indeed received imperial powers in 23 B.C.. The information on the enrollment is derived from Luke 2:1, which reads as follows: "...in those days there went out a decree from Caesar Augustus that the whole world should be enrolled."

4.   Nero (37-68 A.D.), who was the fifth Roman emperor (54-68 A.D.), is in fact known to have granted more independence to the Senate, in the first five years of his rule, under the influence of his tutor, the Stoic philosopher Seneca, and of the prefect of the praetorian guard, Burrus. Eventually, it was his subsequent extravagance, hystrionic conduct and irresponsibility that stirred the indignation of the Senate that ultimately condemned him to die a slave's death, and so Nero was obliged to flee the city. On the other hand, Domitian

(51-96 A.D.) did indeed terrorize the more prominent
members of the Senate during the later part of his rule
(81-96), and particularly those of his opponents who
were known for their Stoic views. His hostility towards
the senators, though, should not be interpreted as an
indiscriminate rejection of any political advice. It is
a historical fact that he did not suspend his own council (consilium) of close advisers that included among
its members citizens of senatorial rank. As elsewhere
in the treatise, Fortescue's historical accuracy is not
to be taken for granted.

5.   The reference is to Frederick III of Habsburg (1415-
1493) who became Holy Roman Emperor in 1452, and whose
possessions, inherited from his father, were limited to
Inner Austria. Fortescue sees continuity where in fact
there was none: between the social and political institutions of Republican and later Imperial Rome, on the
one hand, and those of the Holy Roman Empire, on the
other. His false perception could have been enforced by
a series of factors among which the wide-spread use of
the Roman law, on the Continent in particular, and the
fact that Frederick was crowned Holy Roman Emperor by
the pope in Rome. In short, there could be no resem-
blance between the Roman Senate and Fortescue's council
of experts. The actual purpose of this chapter is to
produce a precendent by means of which to strengthen
his argument in favour of the need and importance of
competent counsel for any head of government.

6.   See DE REGIMINE, 4:11 and 20, to a degree, where
Ptolemy of Lucca discusses among other things the importance of qualified counsel in the running of political
and military affairs, with reference to the Athenians
and Lacedemonians. As in other instances, Fortescue is
vague about his sources. The image of Athens reduced to
the status of a village must have been a commonplace of
his time when scholars could not have failed to compare
not only Rome and Athens, but also the Athens of Plato
and Aristotle to the town of their day.

Chapter 17

1.   Here Fortescue brings in a new factor in the relationship between the council of experts and the king as regards the distribution of offices, namely, unanimity of opinion for the distribution to be suspended.

2.   See Chapter 14, above. In addition, Fortescue underlines the need of what may be considered a period of probation in the service of the crown as a precondition for regular appointment.

3.   The texts both of Plummer's (1885:150) and Clermont's (1869:471) read: "guard of officers". It has been changed to "body of officers" in order to make clear Fortescue's notion of a broader retinue of servants of the crown, capable of fulfilling administrative, military and police functions at the command of the monarch, or when necessary, of his deputies.

4.   Fortescue's bailiff concomitantly fulfills functions related to the local administration of justice **and** those of a manorial bailiff, albeit royal.

5.   This is less a recommendation in favour of a national militia made up of reservists, than a jab at the knightly class and its reluctance, or inability, to fulfill its traditional military obligations towards the king.

6.   See Chapter 15, above, where Fortescue raises the issue of one man and one office, while talking about the members of the king's council of experts. Its wide application would have without doubt expanded the public administrative apparatus. Its efficiency could have improved in the process, too, to the extent of its ability to keep in check the influence and pressure exerted by the local magnates.

7.   That is to say, the crown prince or heir apparent, in his qualities of Prince of Wales, Duke of Cornwall and Earl of Chester.

8.   "...still others a hundred marks" is missing from the Clermont edition. (Works, vol. I, p. 471)

9.   The Clermont edition reads: "forty shillings and ten pence", instead. (Works, vol. I, p. 471)

10. The term "yeoman" refers to a junior officer or re-
tainer of the crown with official functions. Ideally,
according to Fortescue's calculations, such a yeoman
might derive sufficient income for his status out of his
office, though not enough to rank him among the gentry.

11. Two trends are shown here to concur and result into
the accummulation of offices by individuals: one was the
crown's penury, and the other, the prospect of a "fair
income" which offices could bring to those who had no
scruples to squeeze them dry, so to speak, particularly
whenever royal salaries were nominal or uncertain. The
former trend led the monarch to load with offices particularly his next of kin, in lieu of payment for services rendered or to be rendered, and which the latter
could hardly decline even when hard pressed for cash.
Besides, to vest one and the same person with more than
one office was cheaper for the crown, because it reduced
its administrative costs. See also Wolffe (1971:98).

12. In virtue of the king's right to claim the assis-
tance of his subjects within the borders of their counties, and in case of sudden invasion of the country,
outside the particular counties.

13. ...Nemo potest duobus dominis servire (Matt. 6:24).

14. The Clermont edition adds: "in less might...".
(Works, vol. I, p. 472)

15. One of them was the notorious conflict between the
Earl of Devonshire and Sir William Bonville, which might
have affected Fortescue in more than one way, both as a
native of that region with vested interests in it, and
as a representative of the new gentry.

16. The Clermont edition adds: "...or forest". (Works,
vol. I, p. 472)

Chapter 18

1. On corodies see note 3 to Chapter 15. What Fortescue
adds here is the need to consult the council with regard
to their distribution. He seems to. treat them as any

other crown grant, in order to discourage abuse, and
secure equity instead, on the premise that even in the
case of royal foundations, resources were limited and
in an unavoidable state of fluctuation.

2.   It refers to lay clerks or choristers and musicians
who were not subject to any pledge to celibacy and other
monastical rigours, as well as to menial clerks and
servants, who generally speaking, were less likely to
find security in old age on their own. That Fortescue
takes a whole chapter to raise the question of what to
us appears to be the social security of a specific
social group, namely the retired civil servants with no
private income, points to the urgency of the question
in his time.

Chapter 19

1.   To alienate in mortmain meant that the whole patrimony was to be turned into the property of the nation
as corporation, in perpetuity and for such public purposes which included the reproduction of the monarchical
system of government.

2. Once again Fortescue redefines the crown patrimony
as the nation's inalienable property in the custody of
the king. To reinforce his point, he resorts to an ecclesiastical comparison, putting nation and religious
foundation side by side, and comparing parliament with
the assembly of a monastic community. It is doubtful
whether his insistence reproduces the commons' alleged
desire that the king should live of his own. Rather it
seems to be his own aspiration to rebuild the authority
of the crown on a more durable basis. He might have been
influenced in his insistence, to a degree, by his experience of French realities: in that country, the domains
of the crown were indeed inalienable.

3.   Here Fortescue seems to revert to his earlier idea
of the endowment of the crown by parliament, rather than
through permanent and universal taxation.

4. See Chapter 4, above.

86

5. Perhaps even Aristotle with his idea of happiness, whom Fortescue might have had in mind when detailing his own idea of public good.

6. Plummer (1885:94-96) draws one's attention to the fact that two of the MSS which he had seen read "Henry VI", instead, while others were mutilated at this point or missing the part altogether. Even if originally, Fortescue's intention had been to compile a treatise on government for the edification of his pupil, Prince Edward, king Henry VI's son, and on the experience of Henry's reign, it is very likely that the end-product was dedicated to the king who spared his life, and gave him a second chance, so to speak, namely Edward IV. The changes and mutilations may have been the intervention of the censorship in the age of the Tudors who systematically built up a cult of the Lancastrian dynasty, keen as they were on dynastic continuity as a means of legitimizing their own claims to the crown at the expense of the House of York.

7. The Clermont edition goes on as follows: "Therefore God continue his grace and person in long life with increase, in honour and magnificence, to his heart's desire and wealth of this realm'. (Works, vol.I, p. 474)

Chapter 20

1. This chapter is a summary of the payment-for-service system which should regulate the relationship between crown and subjects. Parliament is to assume a greater role in and share of responsibility for the preservation of the patrimony of the crown.

2. To discourage the false impression that land granted in that way was inheritable.

3. In other words, to grant part of the income, in kind or in cash, deriving from the property in question, at pleasure.

4. ...de avisamento consilii sui.

5. It is a tactical move on Fortescue's part to conclude

the treatise by insisting on the positive role that the
council of experts would have in the restauration and
preservation of the monarch's authority. Implicitly, he
reaffirms his own utility to the crown.

6.   The Clermont edition adds: "And God save the king".
(Works, vol.I, p. 474)

(ADMONITION IN SEVEN ARTICLES) *

Here follow, in the form of articles certain recommendations sent by My Lord Prince to the Earl of Warwick, his father-in-law, to be shown and conveyed by him to King Henry, his father, and to his Council, on the understanding that the same recommendations, or such like that may be thought expedient for the public good of the Realm, may be practised and put to use.

1. First, many of the lords and other men of lower estate, which in this time of the King's great trouble have done him good service to their great costs and charges, and other of his faithful subjects, which for his sake and their true acquittal have suffered great harm personally and lost their assets, will now sue His Highness for rewards and compensation for the harms suffered. As much as reason, liberality, and in short, royal munificence allow it, their requests should be granted; yet, if by such consideration, the King gives to one man and not to another, which for similar reason ought to be rewarded, it would give rise to great discontent among his people. Likewise, some may obtain rewards greater than they deserve, by inopportune suit and partial means, and still show their disatisfaction, saying that they have received too little. Furthermore, other men may get too little or right nothing, as they lack the means to reach the King. Therefore, it is thought good that all such rewards and compensations be deferred until a council is established. Then, the supplications of all such persons may be sent by the king to the said council where the merits of every man may be impartially examined. The coun-

cil may first consider what patrimony the king has for the maintenance of his estate, and how what is left may be distributed among such as have well deserved, so that the King by reason of liberality and rewards does not lose or diminish his patrimony in such a way that would compel him to live off his commons and the Church to his infamy and the withdrawal of his subjects' hearts from him, which thing is not God's will. And then, when the King is fully advised by the council about all such supplications, he may so reward every man as he deserves and the King's domain allows it. Were this order observed, then no man may quarrel with His Highness, the King, and the lords or any other about the person of the King as they are wont to do.

2. It is thought good that it should please the King to establish a council of twelve spiritual men and twelve temporal men, of the wisest and most impartial that can be chosen in all the land. That alongside them, four spiritual and four temporal lords, or less should be chosen every year. That the King should not greatly alter the law of his realm, nor give land, fee, office or benefice before he has made his intent known to and examined by that council and has heard their advice on the matter. That may in no way restrain his power, liberty or prerogative. Thus the King should not be counselled by men of his Chamber, his household, or others who cannot advise him. The public good shall be administered by wise men to the prosperity and honour of the land, to the safety and welfare of the King, and to the security of all those who might be about his person, and whom the people have often slain for the bad advice they gave to their sovereign lord. The twenty-four councillors may in no way accept fee, clothing or rewards, or be in any man's service, but do as the justices of the law. Many other articles need be added here, which are too long to be mentioned. Nevertheless, it is thought that the high officers,

such as the Chancellor, the Treasurer, the Lord
Privy Seal, the Judges, the Barons of the Exchequer
and the Clerk of the Rolls may take part in the
council whenever they come to it or the said twenty-
four and the eight lords will desire their presence.
3. It might be thought that the establishment of
such a council would be a new and heavy charge for
the King, when it is remembered how the old council
in England, made up mostly of great lords, attended
more to their own matters than to the good, universal
profit, while professing to be of the council, and
were as much charge to the King as this council will
be, but of no such profit. For this council shall
almost continuously examine and labour upon the
political good will of the land, to see to it that
it makes provisions that no money should be taken
out of the realm and how bullion could be brought in;
how merchandise and commodities of the land may keep
their prices and value, that foreigners should not
devalue the commodities growing in the land, and such
other points of policy. Likewise, how the law may be
firmly observed and reformulated there where it is
defective to the greatest good and security of the
wealth of this, as of any other land. It is true that
of late, some temporal lord has been given much more
property in yearly value than will pay the wages of
all the new council. Likewise, the spiritual men of
this new council will not need wages as high as those
of the temporal men who must leave a household to
their wives, children and servants in their counties,
whenever they attend to council, or else take them
along, a thing which the spiritual men need not do.
On that consideration, the spiritual men in the
Court of Parliament in Paris receive but three hundred crowns, whereas the temporal men have four
hundred.
4. Before the king makes any grant of any part of
his patrimony, it is necessary to assign a certain
revenue in particular for the King's house, for his

chapel and for his wardrobe; and other revenue for
the payment of his courts, his council and all the
other ordinary charges, in such a way that no part
of it be rescinded for any other use until their
yearly payment is due. Any patent that is so made as
to put to any other use any part of that revenue
should be rendered void and of no effect. Likewise,
no patent should be made in inheritance of any part
of the King's patrimony by whatever title it had come
into his possession, without the assent of his Parliament. Nor should any be made for term of life,
or years equal to the term of life, without the
advice of his council, save such patents as shall be
made of farms by the Treasurer of England, bailiffs,
or other officers that have the power to improve the
King's patrimony. The Chancellor who happens to seal
any contrary patent, shall lose his office and for-
feit all his temporal property in favour of the King,
and the patent should be voided. Furthermore, any
Chancellor should be punished likewise if he affixes
the seal on any other patent for any matter, or if
he reveals the way in which that matter was discussed
and the conclusion of its deliberation in the King's
council. If the matter discussed has met with the
approval of the council, the Chacellor may write in
the patent which he will make about it that it has
been passed with the advice and consent of the council, or else he may leave out these words and write
in the patent only that the matter has been deliberated in the King's council.
5.   Whenever there is sufficient revenue to make
payments for the King's household, its expenses shall
always be paid with ready money. Thenceforward, those
expenses shall be so reasonable that the fourth
part of the old expenses of the same household will
be saved yearly. Thereby, the king shall always have
the market at his gate, to his great profit, and so
much more profit to the poor people; and to the
singular pleasure of God who has forgiven no prince

for his debts incurred where victuals are concerned. That is why all the other kings always pay ready money for their foodstuffs.

6. It is thought proper that the King should give none of his offices, not even a parkership, to any man who is not the King's servant, and that each and every officer of his be sworn that he is in no other man's service, nor has or will take from any other man pension, fee or clothing while he is serving the King. Then the King will have the undiminished power of his land which is administered mostly by his officers, as it had been before these days. The King shall then more than reward with offices such as ought to be rewarded without diminishing the revenues of the crown. Still it would be good that no man might hold two offices, except the servants and officers of the king's household, who whenever they deserve it, may have a parkership or other such office that they may adequately keep through a deputy. The deputy then shall be made to swear to serve none other but his master that serves the King. In like form, the King may reward his temporal councillors with such offices when he so wills. It is also likely that he will profer upon the spiritual members of his council such benefices as they will be worthy of.

7. Considering the fact that the King is in great poverty now and may not yet sustain the expenses of as large a household as he once kept, nor is he yet provided with plate and other household furnishings suitable to him and corresponding to his estate, and also that the costs incurred by the instauration of his rule will be greater than anyone can estimate with certainty, it is thought appropriate that it should please His Highness to forbear the keeping of his great and worshipful household during all this first year. During all this time, he should be in such a safe place or places that His Most Noble Grace can think best for his health and pleasure,

with few people and without taking back any of the servants of his old household, during all that year, but only those which he needs to. Because, if he takes any of them back within that time, the rest will grow discontent for having been left out. And even those that have thus been taken back will not forego inopportune suits to have all their old fellowship restored, which will be troublesome and a great nuisance to the King and to all those around him during that year.

(After the Yelverton MS No.35, published by Charles Plummer in 1885)

* The MS from which Plummer reproduced this text bore no title whatsoever.

HE WHO REIGNS POLITICALLY IS HERE ADVISED TO GOVERN ROYALLY IN CERTAIN CASES.

Again, O King, you who govern politically, govern your people royally, too, when occasion demands it. For it is not every case that will admit of being comprised in the statutes and customs of your kingdom; wherefore, such as remain are left to your discretion. For you deal with all criminal matters according to your will and pleasure, and mitigate or remit all punishments, provided only you can do so without damage to your subjects or offence against the customs and statutes of your kingdom. Equity (epikaia)[1] too is left to your sagacity, lest the strictness of the words of the law, confounding its intent, should hurt the common good. In this way, the law forbidding the ascent of the walls of the city is judged not to have been broken by the man, who mounting the walls without licence, drove back the enemy rushing in of a sudden and who would have otherwise taken the town. For on that occasion the observance of the law would have swallowed up the law along with its authors. Nor would those Maccabees, who were slaughtered on the sabbath day, have been despisers of the Commandment which prescribed without condition the observance of the sabbath, although they had gone forth on the sabbath day from the caverns in which they had been hiding and routed their insulting enemies.(I Maccabees,2).[2] Equity, as Aegidius Romanus says, is indulgence above what is just, for human nature always begs for pardon. This virtue, as the Philosopher says in the Fifth Book of the Ethics,[3] does not detract from legal

*justice. For epikaia is so called from epi, which is
above or praise, and kala (l being changed into i),
which is lax, as it were a super-laudable relaxation
of the strictness of law.* [4] *Hence that superior authority is held to have absolute power, not indeed
to violate a perfect law, but rather to fulfill a
law of his own kingdom by reason of the law of nature, which is natural equity. For often, the written
law lies as it were dead under a covering of words,
though no wholly lifeless, and then the Prince, by
means of equity, rouses its vital spirit as if from
sleep, as a physician relieves a stupefied patient
in a syncope, and so the saying of the Gospel may
then be used concerning two laws reposing under one
covering:'There shall be two in one bed; and one
shall be taken, and the other left'.* [5] *Likewise,
often in such a case, the office of a good prince,
who is called a living law, supplies the deficiency
of the written law, which like a dead thing, con-
tinues always immovable. Whence the Philosopher says,
not without cause, that a kingdom is better governed
by the best king than by the best law. But let a
king ruling politically ever beware, lest by repudi-
ating such laws of his own kingdom as are pregnant
with justice, he enacts new laws without consulting
the chief men of his kingdom, or brings in foreign
laws, so that, by refusing for the future to live
politically, he oppresses his peoples with his royal
justice.* [6]

HERE ARE EXPLAINED CERTAIN CASES IN
WHICH A POLITICAL RULER WILL OF
NECESSITY GOVERN ROYALLY

*Nevertheless, there are often cases and very many of
them, in which it is sometimes right and expedient
for a king governing politically to act royally* [7]
against some of his people, in cases such as when his

people have risen in arms against him, or a foreign
nation has invaded his kingdom, and when time does
not allow to do everything which the necessity of re-
sisting and repelling attack requires in due form and
by process of the laws which prevail in that kingdom
in time of peace. Wherefore that king will be at
liberty at his own will to take the sons of his
subjects and set them in his chariots and make them
riders in his chariots, and do everything else which
the Prophet warned the people of Israel was the right
of the king. For as the physician takes care of the
sick man, so does every king of his kingdom; for as
disease is the weakness of bodies, so vice is the
weakness of souls. A physician often binds a sick man
labouring under a cancer or a gnawing disease, lest
the sufferer, impatient of the bitterness of the
medicine, flies from his own safety; and sometimes
the surgeon cuts off the affected limb, when he
cannot save the rest of the body by any other means;
nor does the physician or surgeon err, provided he
restores the sick man to health, though maimed. So
neither does the good king err who, in a time when
such commotion has arisen in his kingdom, wastes the
goods of his subjects or exposes some of them to
inevitable perils, or oppresses others with burdens
and toils for the safety of the kingdom which otherwise he cannot preserve. Since art, as said above,
imitates nature and nature works everything for the
best, and the art of living holds the primacy among
all arts in so far as all other arts refer to it,
and as nature suffers the human body to be mutilated
by the surgeon rather than perish outright and impels
the several members to expose themselves to blows
rather than allow their head to be endangered, so
rather than the king, who is the head of the kingdom,
be allowed to perish, his subjects must be exposed
to danger; and since the king, as St. Thomas says, [8]
is given for the kingdom and not the kingdom for him,
in so far as he is related to the kingdom as the

thing caused to the cause, he ought to surrender himself to all sorts of dangers rather than let the kingdom perish. Therefore, when the foregoing is considered, it is not the dignity or state of a king reigning only royally, or for that matter, of a king presiding over his people both royally and politically, that sets one of them above the other, but only the goodness and the justice of the ruler. For the likeness which their dignity has to the governance of God makes them equal, yet individually, those kings are often unlike in respect of those qualities whereby they are assimilated to the Divine actions. Therefore, clap your hands, you subjects of a king ruling royally, under a good sovereign, whenever there is one like that. Otherwise, you need mourn when an insolent or grasping king rules over you. And you, subjects of a king presiding royally and politically over his kingdom, console yourselves in this respect: would your king be equally arrogant, he has not a loose rein for it, [9] *like the other.*

(Chaps. XXIV & XXV of ON THE LAW OF NATURE)

---

1. $\epsilon\pi\iota\epsilon\iota\kappa\epsilon\iota\alpha$ comes from Aristotle's Nicomachean Ethics, V,x.
2. Here is an instance of Fortescue's condensation of the incidents related in the Apocrypha.
3. Chichester Fortescue, who is the author of the English translation of DE NATURA, identifies the source as De Regimine Principum, III,ii,23.
4. This is another sample of Fortescue's etymological fantasy. He might have used the trick to hide his ignorance of classical Greek.
5. Luke, 17,34-35.
6. ...jus regale.
7. ...regaliter.
8. See note 3 to Chapter 8 above.
9. That is, free scope.

SELECT BIBLIOGRAPHY

The Works of Sir John Fortescue, col. by Thomas
     (Fortescue), Lord Clermont. 2 vols., London, 1869.
Fortescue, Sir John: The Governance of England, ed. by
     C. Plummer, Oxford, 1885.
Fortescue, Sir John: De Laudibus Legum Angliae, ed.
     and trans. by S.B. Chrimes. London, 1942.

Anglo, S.: Machiavelli - a Dissection. London, 1969.
Allmand, C.T.: Lancastrian Normandy 1415-1450. Oxford,
     1983.
Augustin, St.: De Civitate Dei, ed. and trans. by
     J.W.C. Wand. London, 1963.
Aristotle: Nicomachean Ethics, trans. by M. Oswald.
     Indianapolis, 1962.
Aristotle: Politics, ed. and trans. by E. Barker.
     Oxford, 1946.
Baldwin, J.F.: The King's Council in England during
     the Middle Ages. Oxford, 1913.
Bean, J.M.W.: The Decline of English Feudalism
     1215-1540. Manchester, 1968.
Bean, J.M.W.: From Lord to Patron. Manchester, 1989.
Baedae: Opera Historica in Two Volumes. Vol. I: Ec-
     clesiastical History of the English Nation,
     trans. by J.E. King. London and New York, 1930.
Bellamy, J.G.: Crime and Public Order in England
     during Later Middle Ages. London, 1973 .
Bernardus, De Cura Rei Famuliaris (Sic), ed. by J.R.
     Lumby. London, New York, 1965 c1870.
Bodin, J.: Six Books of the Commonwealth, ed. and
     trans. by M.J. Tooley. Oxford, 1955.
Bodin, J.: On Sovereignty, ed. and trans. by J.H.
     Franklin. Cambridge, 1922.
Bolton, J.L.: The Medieval English Economy, 1150-1500.
     London, 1980.
Boulton, A.J.D.: The Knights of the Crown (1325-1520).
     New York, 1987.
Bracton, H. de: De Legibus et Consuetudinibus Angliae,

ed. by T. Twiss. Vol. II. Buffalo, 1990 c1879

Bridbury, A.R.: England and the Salt Trade in the
    Later Middle Ages. Oxford, 1955.

British Government and Administration, ed. by H.
    Hearder and H.R. Loyn. Cardiff, 1974.

Brown, A.L.: The Governance of Late Medieval England
    1272-1461. London and Stanford, 1989.

Cambridge History of Medieval Political Thought,
    c.350-c.1450, ed. by J.H. Burns. Cambridge, 1988.

Carus-Wilson, E.M. and Coleman, O.: England's Export
    Trade, 1275-1547. Oxford, 1963.

Chrimes, S.B.: English Constitutional Idea in the 15th
    Century. Cambridge, 1936.

Chrimes, S.B.: Henry VII. London, 1972.

Chrimes, S.B.: An Introduction to the Administrative
    History of Medieval England, 3rd ed. Oxford, 1966.

Chrimes, S.B.: Lancastrians, Yorkists and Henry VII,
    2nd ed. London, 1967.

Colvin, H.M. et al.: The History of the King's Works:
    the Middle Ages, 2 vols. London, 1963.

Commynes, P.: The Memoirs for the Reign of Louis XI,
    1461-1483, trans. by M. Jones. Harmondsworth, 1972.

Constable, R.: Prerogativa Regis, ed. by S.E. Thorne.
    New Haven, 1949.

Dobson, R.B.: The Church, Politics and Patronage in
    the 15th Century. Gloucester, 1984.

Dyer, C.: Standards of Living in the Later Middle Ages.
    Cambridge and New York, 1989.

Économies et sociétés au Moyen Age. Paris, 1973.

Favier, J.: Finance et fiscalité au bas Moyen Age.
    Paris, 1971.

Ferguson, J.: English Diplomacy, 1422-1461. Oxford,
    1972.

Fifteenth Century England, 1399-1509, ed. by S.B.
    Chrimes, C.D. Ross and R.A. Griffiths. Manchester,
    1972. (Pugh)

Geoffrey of Monmouth: Historia Regum Britanniae, trans.
    by R.E. Jones. London, 1929.

Gillespie, J.L.:"Sir John Fortescue's Concept of Royal
    Will" in Nottingham Medieval Studies 23(1979),
    pp. 47-65.

Gilmore, M.P.: Argument from Roman Law in Polit-
    ical Thought, 1200-1600. Cambridge MA 1941.
Goodman, A.: The New Monarchy: England 1471-1534.
    Oxford and New York, 1988.
Goodman, A.: The War of the Roses - Military Activity
    and English Society, 1452-1497. London, 1981.
Griffiths, R.A.: The Reign of Henry VI. London, 1979.
Guenée, B.: L'Occident aux XIVe et XVe siècles. Les
    états, 4th ed. Paris, 1991.
Guenée, B.: States and Rulers in Later Medieval Europe,
    trans. by J. Vale. Oxford, 1985.
Glanvill: The Treatise on the Laws and Customs of the
    Realm of England, ed. by G.D.G. Hall. London, 1965.
Hanson, D.W.: From Kingdom to Commonwealth. Cambridge
    MA, 1970.
Harris, G.L.: Cardinal Beaufort. Oxford, 1988.
Hastings, M.: The Court of Common Pleas in the 15th
    -Century England. Ithaca NY, 1947.
Hatcher, J.: Plague, Population and the English
    Economy, 1348-1530. London, 1977.
Helmholz, R.H.: Canon Law and the Law of England.
    London and Ronceverte, 1987.
Hilton, R.H.: The English Peasantry in the Later Middle
    Ages. Oxford, 1975.
Holdsworth, W.S.: A History of English Law, vol. I (7th
    ed.). London, 1956. Vols. II and III (3rd ed.).
    Aberdeen, 1922-1923.
Jacob, E.F.: The Fifteenth Century. Oxford, 1961.
Jolliffe, J.E.A.: The Constitutional History of
    Medieval England, 2nd ed. Edinburgh, 1948.
Justinian's Institutes, trans. by P. Birks and G.
    McLeod. London, 1987.
Ives, E.W.: The Common Lawyers of Pre-Reformation
    England. Cambridge, 1983.
Kaemper, R.W.: War, Justice and Public Order. England
    and France in the Later Middle Ages. Oxford, 1988.
Kantorowicz, E.H.: The King's Two Bodies. Princeton,
    1957.
Kendall, P.M.: Warwick the Kingmaker. London, 1957.
Knowles, M.D.: The Monastic Order in England (940-
    1216), 2nd ed. Cambridge, 1966.

Lander, J.R.: Conflict and Stability in 15th-Century
    England, 3rd ed. London, 1977.
Lander, J.R.: Crown and Nobility 1450-1509. Montreal,
    1976.
Lander, J.R.: Government and Community in England,
    1450-1509. Cambridge MA, 1980.
Lander, J.R.: The Wars of the Roses. New York, 1990.
Lawrence, C.H.: English Church and the Papacy in the
    Middle Ages. London, 1965.
Litzen, V.: A War of Roses and Lilies. Helsinki, 1971.
Lloyd, I.H.: The English Wool Trade in the Middle Ages.
    Cambridge, 1977.
Loades, D.M.: Politics and the Nation, 1450-1660.
    London, 1974.
Lyon, B.D.: Constitutional and Legal History of
    Medieval England, 2nd ed. London, 1980.
Lyon, B.D.: From Fief to Indenture. Cambridge MA, 1957.
McFarlane, K.B.: The Nobility of Later Medieval
    England. Oxford, 1973.
Maritain, J.: The Person and the Common Good, trans.
    by J.T. Fitzgerald. London, 1948.
Meinecke, F.: Machiavellism - the Doctrine of Raison
    d'État, trans. by D. Scott. London, 1957.
Mertes, K.: The English Noble Household 1250-1600.
    Oxford, 1988.
Miskimin, H.A.: Money and Power in the 15th-Century
    France. New Haven, 1984.
Munro, J.H.: Wool, Cloth and Gold. Toronto, 1972.
Myers, A.R.: The Household of Edward IV. Manchester,
    1959.
Newhall, R.A.: Muster and Review. Cambridge MA, 1940.
Oakley, F.: Natural Law, Conciliarism and Consent in
    the Late Middle Ages. London, 1984.
Ogilvie, C.: The King's Government and the Common Law.
    Oxford, 1958.
Paston Letters and Papers of the 15th Century, ed. by
    N. Davis. Oxford, 1971.
Plucknett, T.F.T.: A Concise History of Common Law,
    5th ed. London, 1956.
Plucknett, T.F.T.: English Constitutional History,
    5th ed. London, 1960.

Post, G.: Studies in Medieval Legal Thought. Princeton NJ, 1964.

Postan, M.M.: Medieval Economy and Society. London, 1972.

Powicke, M.R.: Military Obligation in Medieval England. Oxford, 1962.

Profession, Vocation and Culture in Later Medieval England, ed. by C.H. Clough. Liverpool, 1982.

Richardson, H.G. and Sayles, G.O.: The Governance of Medieval England. Edinburgh, 1963.

Richmond, C.F.:"English Naval Power in the 15th Century" in History. London, vol. LII(1967), pp.1-15.

Roskell, J.S.: The Commons and the Speakers in English Parliaments, 1376-1523. Manchester, 1965.

Roskell, J.S.: Parliament and Politics in Late Medieval England, 3 vols. London, 1981-1983.

Ross, C.: Edward IV. London, 1974.

Russel-Major, J.: The Monarchy, the States and the Aristocracy in Renaissance France. London, 1988.

Salzman, L.: Building in England to 1540. Oxford, 1952.

Sanders, I.J.: Feudal Military Service in England. Oxford, 1956.

Sayles, G.O.: The Court of King's Bench in Law History. London, 1959.

Sayles, G.O.: The Functions of the Medieval Parliament of England. London, 1988.

Schramm, P.E.: A History of the English Coronation. Oxford, 1937.

Social and Political Ideas of Some Great Thinkers of the Renaissance and the Reformation, ed. by F.J.C. Hearnshaw. New York, 1949.

Steel, A.B.: The Receipt of the Exchequer, 1377-1485. Cambridge, 1954.

Storey, R.L.: The End of the House of Lancaster. London, 1966.

Strayer, J.R.: On the Medieval Origins of the Modern State. Princeton, 1970.

Swanson, R.N.: Church and Society in Late Medieval England, 2nd ed. Oxford and Cambridge MA, 1993.

Taswell-Langmead, T.P.: English Constitutional History, 11th ed. London, 1960.

Thomas Aquinas, St.: On Kingship to the King of Cyprus,
    ed. by I.Th. Eschmann. Toronto, 1949.

Thomas Aquinas, St.: Regimiento de Principes de Santo
    Tomás de Aquino, ed. and trans. by L. Getino.
    Valencia, 1931.

Thompson, A.H.: The English Clergy and Their Organ-
    ization in the Later Middle Ages. Oxford, 1947.

Thrupp, S.: The Merchant Class of Medieval London 1300-
    1500. Chicago, 1948.

Tuck, A.: Crown and Nobility, 1272-1461. London, 1985.

Wilkinson, B.: Constitutional History of England in the
    15th Century, 1399-1485. New York, 1964.

Wilks, M.J.: The Problem of Sovereignty in the Later
    Middle Ages. Cambridge, 1963.

Wolffe, B.P.: The Crown Lands, 1461-1536. London, 1970.

Wolffe, B.P.: The Royal Demesne in English History.
    London, 1971.

Wolffe, B.P.: Henry VI, 1981.

INDEX

The index combines proper names and topical entries
from the text proper, the Appendices and the Notes. The
Introduction has not been indexed.